DATE DUE

THE FREEMAN JOURNAL

THE FREEMAN JOURNAL:

The Infantry in the Sioux Campaign of 1876

Edited by George A. Schneider

With an Introduction by John M. Carroll

Presidio Press
SAN RAFAEL • CALIFORNIA

The Freeman Journal appears with the permission of the Yale University Library.

PRESIDIO PRESS
1114 Irwin Street
San Rafael, Calif. 94901

Library of Congress Catalog Card No. 76-29573
ISBN: 0-89141-060-0

Printed in the United States of America.

Designed by Marjorie Weiss
Mulch Press
Northampton, Massachusetts

Presidio Press
SAN RAFAEL • CALIFORNIA

CONTENTS

MAPS AND ILLUSTRATIONS

INTRODUCTION

INTRODUCTION

Just how and why the Freeman journal has escaped full publication to date is a mystery to me. Dustin (No. 396) says of it: "A very important historical document. A revealing manuscript." Of course he was referring to only that portion of the journal from June 12 to July 26, 1876, and not the whole journal, which covers the period from March 21 to October 6, 1876. Mike Koury, author of *Diaries of the Little Big Horn* (Old Army Press, 1968), said of it: "Freeman's diary should be read carefully. It contains much of interest and reveals much of the inner turmoil that histories of the Sioux War of 1876 seem [to be] unaware [of]." So how has it escaped publication? One answer may be in Koury's comment in his book when he stated: "Freeman uses initials and at times they cannot be traced. The statements often leave you with a great deal of curiosity." If this is the reason, then the problem has been solved.

At last a student of the battle and a Custer scholar, George A. Schneider, has done much to unravel most of the mysteries contained within the journal and, except for two instances, all the abbreviations and initials have been identified. It is a masterful task well done, and one which should go a long way toward filling some of the voids in that vast body of literature relating to Custer and the battle.

George Schneider, a retired chief warrant officer and a 32-year veteran of the army, is presently spending his time in research and writing at his home in Old Bridge, New Jersey. A longtime lover of military history, George is a collector of such artifacts, specializing in military firearms predating the twentieth century. Upon retirement, George returned to school and completed his B.S. degree in military science at the University of Maryland; he received his M.A. degree in history from the State University of New York at Oneonta, New York. His masters thesis was titled "Fact and Fancy at the Little Big Horn," a study of the pictures and paintings depicting that famed battle. Upon completion of his M.A. degree, George accepted the position of curator at the Patton Museum at Fort Knox, Kentucky, a post which he filled for six years until his second retirement. He has been published in the *Southwest Historical Review*, the *New York Westerners Posse* and the *Little Big Horn Associates Newsletter*.

When one reads Dustin's entry in his Custer bibliographic checklist concerning the Freeman journal, it is easy to fall into a trap; one could be led to believe that the entire portion of the diary (June 12-July 26, 1876) was completely footnoted by him. This is far from the truth; only a very few notes were made by him, and because of the curiosity his insinuation might cause, I feel it important to record these notes and thereby preserve them. They are historically important, though not very revealing. His notes to the Freeman journal are:

First note preceding the June 12 entry: "The diary begins on June 12, 1876 so far as herein quoted. At that time Gibbon's command was marching up the Yellowstone and had camped for the night on the 11th, just above the mouth of Mud Creek which enters the Yellowstone six or seven miles below the Tongue, on the north side of the former."

Note to June 12 entry: "The 'Custer fight' mentioned took place on the north bank of the Yellowstone, above the mouth of the Tongue."

Note to June 29 entry with reference to the entry by Freeman which had pencil lines drawn through it: "[deleted] probably because they were out of place. Benteen, seeing how matters stood, joined his force to that of Reno where they fought for some time. In the meantime, one company with the pack train was coming on and took to the bluffs on Custer's trail. As they were raising the bluff they were met by heavy fire and luckily were able to hold their own."

Note to June 12 entry with reference to number of Reno's men killed: "Capt. Freeman is in error in this. Eight or 10 of Reno's men were killed *before* the charge started, and including that number, 29 were killed from the start of the engagement to the time that Reno rallied the battalion on the bluffs."

Note to June 12 entry with reference to the map: "The map referred to is evidently a copy of Maguire's."

Note to June 12 entry with reference to number of men lost in the battle: "The aggregate of loss is naturally inaccurate for several reasons, the chief of which is that almost invariably the full strength of each of Custer's troops was figured whereas seven from each were with the pack train, an aggregate of 35, so often reported 'missing.' The total loss was so far as can be accurately ascertained, including wounded, 322. Therefore, adding the 35 with the packs, Freeman's figures are quite correct as to the total, but only one Assistant Surgeon and one Acting Assistant Surgeon were killed."

Note to July 4 entry: "Sanno was one of the captains in the 7th Infantry. The Crows who had remained were Half-Yellow Face, White Swan and Curly. White Swan was lying in the field hospital very badly wounded."

A final note to the whole of the diary cited in his No. 396 was this: "A number of very interesting facts are brought out as is usual in a diary of this sort, such as the charges against Sanno and Reno's being put under arrest. Much unwritten history."

And that is the extent of Fred Dustin's notes to the Freeman journal as indicated in his checklist. They are not revealing and are nothing much more than bits of common knowledge tinged with a bit of bias, the insinuation of his entry notwithstanding.

George Schneider has done us all a great service in getting this journal into proper and readable form. Our continuing enrichment of facts concerning this famed general and his tragic end at the Little Big Horn — as well as that of his command — has been well served with this expertly edited journal.

JOHN M. CARROLL
New Brunswick, N.J.

THE JOURNAL AND ITS AUTHOR

THE JOURNAL AND ITS AUTHOR

Among the many items of Western Americana reposing in the William Robertson Coe Collection at Yale, none is so certain to excite the interest of Custer enthusiasts as a worn copybook, some seven by five inches, the manuscript diary of Captain Henry B. Freeman, 7th Infantry. A few minutes with the captain's notes and the reader is apt to find himself trudging along with the "Montana Column" of 1876 as it wends its way from Fort Shaw to the Little Big Horn's banks, there to come upon the remnants of Custer's regiment. Then follows march and countermarch in the hunt for Sitting Bull.

There are no polished phrases, merely crisp soldier talk, enlivened now and then by some biting comment – the result of an associate's thoughtless act or similar cause. These observations, while often hypercritical, clothe in human qualities several personalities who otherwise would continue as mere names in history. After reading a few pages of the manuscript, it becomes easy to picture our blue-clad captain, rankled by some untoward incident of the day, as he sits crouched over his journal at twilight or, perhaps, by dim candlelight. Obviously a journal so full of the human touch was compiled for personal use only, providing the writer with an opportunity to "let off steam" on occasion.

Henry Blanchard Freeman was born in Ohio on January 17, 1837, the son of New England parents. While still but a lad he enlisted in the 10th U.S. Infantry and served at Fort Crawford, Wisconsin, until the fact of his minority became known and he was discharged.[1] But the savor of military life had proven zestful, for hardly had Fort Sumter's guns been silenced when Freeman was again in army blue, the first recruit for the 18th U.S. Infantry then being organized within his native state.[2] Four months later and the young soldier was discharged as a first sergeant to accept a second lieutenant's commission in the regular establishment.[3] In the long and bloody struggle ahead the youth was to demonstrate how well he merited that commission, being brevetted for gallantry on two occasions and earning the coveted Congressional Medal of Honor as well.[4]

The Battle of Chickamauga in 1863 saw his regiment badly mauled; Freeman was captured while attempting to rescue a wounded comrade.[5] But even Libby Prison did not take away his spirit, for he was among those who tunneled their way to freedom. Unfortunately, he, like so many of the conspirators, was soon back within those walls. Undaunted, Freeman tried again, again, and yet again. On February 14, 1865, after almost eighteen months of prison life, and on his fourth bid for liberty, he reached the Federal lines – Sherman's army in Georgia – at last.[6] In the decades that followed, Freeman slowly climbed the ladder of promotion while participating in the various Indian disturbances of the Northwest, the Spanish-

---

1. Records of the Pension Bureau, NARS, RG 15, T-288, Roll 163, and Widow's Pension Application No. 1,057,758.

2. Frances Courtney Carrington, *My Army Life and the Fort Phil Kearney Massacre*, Philadelphia, J.B. Lippincott Co., 1910, pp. 197.

3. Register of Enlistments, U.S. Army, NARS, A.G.O. Records, RG 94, vols. 54-55 (A-K), 1859-1863, p. 45, line 183; Francis B. Heitman, *Historical Register and Dictionary of the U.S. Army*, Washington, G.P.O., 1903, I:435-436.

4. Heitman, *loc. cit.*

5. Col. C. A. Woodruff to Hon. J. B. Foraker, U.S. Senate, undated manuscript letter among Service Papers of Henry Blanchard Freeman, NARS, RG 94; Dept. of the Army, *The Medal of Honor*, Washington, G.P.O., 1948, p. 121.

6. Woodruff's letter, *loc. cit.*; *Army and Navy Journal*, LIII:8(Oct. 23, 1915):234, obituary notice of General Freeman; Anson B. Ostrander, *An Army Boy of the Sixties*, Yonkers, N.Y., privately printed, 1924, p. 265.

American War, and the Philippine Insurrection. Finally, on January 17, 1901, a distinguished military career came to a close with the retirement of the seventy-year-old soldier as a brigadier general.[7]

The journal owes its existence to the rather unexpected transfer of command of five companies of the 7th U.S. Infantry from Captain Charles Rawn to Freeman. This force, the nucleus of the "Montana Column," had departed from Fort Shaw, Montana, on St. Patrick's Day, 1876, despite a severe snowstorm. The temperature fell to 20 degrees below zero that night and did not improve much in the days ahead. Snow blindness forced some to leave the column, Captain Rawn being among these, and the command devolved upon Freeman on March 20.[8] The next day the journal was begun.

Other than the journal entries, the copybook has a few recipes [i.e., receipts], unit fund jottings, and a notation concerning a man of the company who had deserted a 14th Infantry unit the previous year.[9] The pad seems to have been intended originally as a recipe [receipt] book; the cover is so inscribed.

The contrast between the handwriting of the recipes [receipts] and that of the journal is rather startling. The former flows in fine Spencerian curves while the latter is little more than a hurried scrawl, often illegible and with frequent resort to initials and non standard abbreviations. There are occasional blottings or water stains. In some instances the ink has seeped through the paper so that the blend on the reverse side mocks interpretation. Time and the ele-

---

7. Heitman, *loc. cit.*

8. "The Journal of James H. Bradley," (hereafter cited as *Bradley*), *Contributions to the Historical Society of Montana,* II (1896):141-143. In 1961, the journal, edited by Edgar I. Stewart, one of today's foremost Custer authorities, was republished as *The March of the Montana Column: A Prelude to the Custer Disaster*, Norman, University of Oklahoma Press. Inasmuch as the former is quite rare today, whereas the latter is generally encountered, references to each will be indicated – that of the 1961 edition enclosed within parenthesis; (12-14).

9. *Muster Roll, Co. H, 7th Infantry, September-October, 1876, NARS, A.G.O., RG 94*, p. 1, identifies this man as Pvt. Richard Parsley, a deserter from Co. F, 14th Inf., who reenlisted as Henry Scott and was assigned to Freeman's Co. H, 7th Inf. Undoubtedly Parsley was recognized by former comrades of the 14th when his original unit moved into the Yellowstone area in August.

ments have taken their toll: here the ink has faded, there a portion of the page is missing. An entire leaf is gone, thus to know what happened between April 11 and 16 it is necessary to consult the diaries of Lieutenants Bradley, English, McClernand, Roe, or Dr. Paulding.

Freeman reveals his physical condition in words and in script. On the days when he was ill, suffered from severe toothache, sleeplessness, or, far worse, the gnawing pangs of homesickness, his hand borders on the indecipherable. Thus fragments of his thoughts still lie hidden among the journal notes.

Although never before published, the manuscript journal is highly regarded by Custeriana authorities. The Dustin Custer Bibliography terms it "a very important historical document, revealing."[10] Edward Eberstadt, writing of the Coe Collection, finds the Freeman manuscript not only better written but of greater value than that of Lieutenant English, and "it gives record of Custer's orders."[11] Unquestionably, Freeman's frankness in commenting upon events and personages renders the journal valuable in other fields as well. It also affords an excellent insight into the thoughts and habits of a frontier military man during the post-Civil War era.

"Sallie," of the diary, was an army bride of 1866 who, in the true tradition of the frontier military, accompanied her soldier-husband on his far-off assignments. During the period of the diary, she and the two Freeman boys remained at Fort Shaw, her husband's home station, and, understandably, Freeman longed to be with his family. (Perhaps this yearning, so evident in the pages of the journal, was a foreboding of things to come. In a few years the elder son would drown while striving to rescue his brother from such a fate.)[12]

---

10. W. A. Graham, *The Custer Myth: A Source Book of Custeriana*, Harrisburg, The Stackpole Co., 1953, p. 396, item 396.

11. *Yale University Library Gazette*, XXIII:2(Oct., 1948):95.

12. *Army and Navy Journal*, XX:19(Dec. 9, 1882):414, notice of death by drowning of Reese Darlington Freeman, son of Captain Freeman, on Dec. 1, while skating on the Minnesota River near Ft. Snelling.

But Freeman's feelings did not interfere with his execution of duty or lessen his interest in the men of his command.

Anson B. Ostrander testifies to the esteem in which Captain Freeman was held by enlisted personnel.[13] Both the Mrs. Carringtons speak warmly of the Freeman hospitality.[14] The sole unfavorable comment uncovered, that of Luther S. Kelly,[15] might easily stem from a misunderstanding as to the proper sphere of the captain's responsibilities. The latter's impatience with negligence and insubordination is clearly evident in the journal's pages. How much this irritability was chargeable to sickness and lack of sleep during the campaign, or to what degree the privations of prison life in an impoverished South were responsible, will never be known.[16]

Identification was established by frequent consultation of Heitman's *Historical Register and Dictionary of the U.S. Army*; from the *Official Army Registers* issued by the Adjutant General's Office from 1875 to 1880; from contemporary Muster Rolls of the respective units; and from other sources, as indicated in the footnotes. Likewise, in editing these papers, repeated reference was made to all available accounts of the "Montana Column." Of particular help was the "Journal of James H. Bradley," either in the original version of 1896 or that of 1961, as edited by Edgar I. Stewart.[17]

Special acknowledgment is due the Yale University Library, particularly to Miss Dorothy W. Bridgewater, for permission to use and publish the Freeman manuscript. Thanks, also, are due the His-

---

13. *An Army Boy of the Sixties*, is replete with references to Captain Freeman, particularly pp. 175-176; also, by the same author, *After Sixty Years*, Seattle, privately printed, 1925, pp. 36-38.

14. Margaret I. Carrington, *AB-SA-RA-KA, Land of Massacre,* Philadelphia, J. B. Lippincott and Co., 1878, p. 238, and Frances Courtney Carrington, *My Army Life and the Fort Phil Kearney Massacre*, pp. 197-198.

15. W. M. Quaife (ed.), *"Yellowstone Kelly," The Memoirs of Luther S. Kelly*, New Haven, Yale University Press, 1926, p. 203.

16. See journal entry of July 19 relating to the suicide of Capt. Lewis Thompson, 2nd Cavalry, who had been imprisoned with Freeman.

17. *The March of the Montana Column: A Prelude to the Custer Disaster*, Norman, University of Oklahoma Press, 1961.

torical Section, Department of the Army, for a copy of the diary of Dr. Holmes Offley Paulding.

Except for obvious errors in spelling or of a similar nature, undoubtedly due to a desire to set down the events of the day and get on with other and more pressing matters, the journal is here presented as it appears today.

GEORGE A. SCHNEIDER

BACKGROUND TO THE LITTLE BIG HORN

BACKGROUND TO THE LITTLE BIG HORN

While Freeman's journal has a special appeal to Custer enthusiasts, those not versed in the lore of the Little Big Horn have not been forgotten. The next few pages summarize the events leading to the battle of June 25, 1876, and include the role of Freeman's battalion of the 7th U.S. Infantry as well as other elements involved.

As the final days of 1875 were tumbling into history, the Indian situation in the Black Hills area was considered somewhat threatening but hardly ominous.[18] Most redmen were making some pretense, at least, of following the "white man's road." An appreciable number, however, remained obdurate and continued in the old ways; these non-agency Indians frequented an area centered about the Powder River country of southern Montana and northern Wyoming. The more defiant not only would not come in for rations but refused to accept the gifts which the "Great White Father" occasionally bestowed upon his red children, particularly, it would seem, upon the least responsive.

---

18. Ellis Paxson Oberholtzer, *A History of the United States Since the Civil War*, III:397-400; LeRoy R. Hafen and Carl Coke Rister, *Western America: The Exploration, Settlement, and Development of the Region Beyond the Mississippi*, New York, Prentice-Hall, 1941, p. 531.

Among the recalcitrants, those of the Uncpapa (Hunkpapa) Sioux, the Oglala Sioux, and the Northern Cheyennes were considered the most troublesome. Their warriors were among the fiercest and most warlike of the tribes north of the Rio Grande.[19] At their head were such natural leaders as Sitting Bull of the Uncpapa Sioux, Crazy Horse of the Oglala, and Two Moon, Little Horse, and White Bull of the Northern Cheyennes. These remained aloof from the whites and lived in the time-honored custom of their race, which custom, unfortunately, required that there be an occasional raid on the neighboring Crows, traditional enemies of the Sioux but long friendly to the whites, plus a foray now and then upon a passing wagon train or a railroad surveying party. These incursions meant *coups* and booty, fame and fortune to the Indian.[20]

Such was the situation when Inspector E. C. Watkins, U.S. Indian Bureau, was sent to investigate the matter and submit a report of his findings and recommendations to the Commissioner of Indian Affairs in Washington. On November 9, 1875, the document was forthcoming; he accused the non-agency Indians of being at the core of the trouble. Because of their location in the best hunting grounds remaining, Mr. Watkins declared, they were rich in horses and robes, were well armed with many breechloading rifles and revolvers, plus the more common bows and arrows. Their independence and arrogance, the inspector felt, were but the result of such wealth, and as their's was the path to glory, their influence was entirely out of proportion to their numerical strength, which he placed at but a few hundred.[21]

---

19. Frederick Webb Hodge, *Handbook of the American Indians North of Mexico*, Washington, Smithsonian Institution, Bureau of American Ethnology Bulletin No. 30, 1905 (reprint, New York, Pageant Books, 1959), I:377; II:578.

20. *44th Congress, 1st Sess., Senate Executive Document No. 52*, Washington, G.P.O., 1876, pp. 3, 10-11; J. P. Dunn, *Massacres of the Mountains: A History of the Indian Wars of the Far West, 1815-1875*, New York, Harper and Bros., 1886 (reprint, New York, Archer House, 1958), pp. 507-510.

21. A résumé of the situation leading to the Sioux War of 1876, including the complete text of the Watkin's report, may be found in *44th Congress, 1st Sess., Senate Executive*

The Indian inspector believed that past efforts to win over the holdouts by peaceful means had proven ineffective. He recommended that now the military, in strength of about a thousand, led by an officer experienced in Indian ways, be given the task of rounding up the unruly and driving them onto the reservations. This, he concluded, would best be accomplished during the winter months, for then the savages were confined to their tepees. Their ponies, too, would be weak as the snow hid the nutritious grasses on which the animals depended.

In line with these findings, the Commissioner ordered the Indian agents to notify their charges not on reservation land to come in by January 31, 1876, on penalty of being considered "hostiles," in which event they would be turned over to the War Department for necessary action. Bureau authorities were determined that the holdouts would follow the "white man's road."

This word reached the Sioux agencies just before Christmas of 1875 and was immediately relayed to the non-agency villages. The winter of 1875-1876 was an unusually severe one. In fact, some of the messengers were unable to return before the deadline, but students of the affair generally concede that other motives besides the weather impelled the intractables to pursue the course they did.[22] No doubt a primary cause was the disdain, sometimes open contempt, in which they held Bureau employees. In the Indian view these spoke much too much, threatened too often, yet seldom acted upon such threats. Then, too, had not the Indian a perfect right to be where he was? It was unceded land, his land! In any event, a handful replied to the effect that they were "too busy" but would think about it, and maybe come in later, in the spring – not so inso-

---

Document No. 52. Also, see Mark H. Brown, *The Plainsmen of the Yellowstone: A History of the Yellowstone Basin*, New York, G. P. Putnam's Sons, 1961, pp. 227-239.

22. Thomas B. Marquis, *Wooden Leg: A Warrior Who Fought Custer*, Lincoln, University of Nebraska Press, 1957 (reprint of the 1931 edition), pp. 159-161; Mark H. Brown, "A New Focus on the Sioux War," *Montana, the Magazine of Western History,* XI:4(Autumn, 1961):76-85.

lent to the native American as it may sound to the ears of others. Most, however, did not deign to reply.

In the meanwhile, on January 18, 1876, the Indian Bureau belatedly telegraphed its agents to halt all sales of arms and ammunition and, three days later, reaffirmed its intention of utilizing the army to enforce Bureau directives. Finally, on February 1, the Secretary of the Interior, under whose control the Indian Bureau came, officially notified the Secretary of War that the deadline had passed with the ultimatum ignored. He therefore requested that action be taken against the hostiles.

Army brass of the period – in fact, all but the most junior of second lieutenants – were veterans of the Civil War, and not a few had been generals in that struggle, at least by brevet. More than a few officers and enlisted men had extensive experience with the redman.

Brevet rank, then quite common, is confusing today, but it was merely a means of conferring honor without cost to the government upon a servant of the Republic who had distinguished himself. It granted what amounted to honorary rank in a grade higher than that in which actually serving, but with no increase in pay. Thus, at this time, George Armstrong Custer, actually a lieutenant colonel of cavalry, was very often referred to as "General," he having been so brevetted and, in addition, had served as a brigadier general and major general of volunteers during the war. This was also true of Colonel John Gibbon, 7th Infantry, and many others with the expedition.[23]

The military decided upon a three-pronged offensive as affording the most promising opportunity of rounding up the non-agency Indians. Brigadier General Alfred H. Terry was to move westward from

---

23. Heitman, I:342,452. Gibbon was an officer of the old school, commanded a corps as early as Gettysburg, and had been brevetted four times. A native of Pennsylvania but appointed to the Military Academy from North Carolina, he had elected to remain loyal to the Union, although three brothers fought in the Confederate ranks. For laudatory remarks on this honest and conscientious, but almost forgotten, soldier, see G. A. Graham, *The Custer Myth*, p. 200, and Mark M. Boatner, *Civil War Dictionary*, New York, David McKay Co., 1959, pp. 340-341.

Fort Abraham Lincoln (near present-day Bismark, N.D.), Brigadier General George Crook would head northward from Fort Fetterman (today's Douglas, Wyo.), while a small force from western Montana, led by Colonel Gibbon, would patrol the Yellowstone to prevent the hostiles from escaping northward across that stream. Upon the arrival of Terry's "Dakota Column," Gibbon's "Montana Column" would unite with it. These forces were to operate simultaneously on a common mission, but it is doubtful if any degree of collaboration was possible between Terry and Crook, for the area was vast and relatively little known, the terrain was rough, and existing communications were poor.[24]

The greatest delay in getting under way was encountered by Terry as three troops of the 7th Cavalry were still on Reconstruction duties in the South. Operational orders issued at Terry's headquarters on February 27 were delayed in transmission to Fort Shaw because of the ugly weather, and for the same reason prompt compliance was impossible.

With the temperature hovering around zero and several inches of snow covering the ground, Companies A, B, H, I, and K, 7th Infantry, the nucleus of the "Montana Column," left Fort Shaw about 10:00 A.M., Friday, March 17. Due to the temporary absence of Colonel Gibbon, Captain Charles C. Rawn exercised command. A battalion of the 2nd Cavalry was scheduled to join the foot soldiers at Fort Ellis, some 180 miles ahead. The combined groups, plus Company E, 7th Infantry, from Camp Baker, would give Gibbon a strength of 456 officers and men, with one 12-pounder Napoleon gun and two .50 caliber Gatling guns.[25]

The strength figure is somewhat deceiving, for military practice at that period called for the establishment of an advanced base on such expeditions. Here wagon trains from the permanent post would discharge their loads, then return to bring up more material to re-

---

24. *Report of the Secretary of War, 1876*, Washington, G.P.O., 1876 (hereafter, *RSW*), pp. 27-30.

25. *Bradley*, p. 164 (50).

plenish that issued. Other wagons, from the field, would pick up stores needed up front. This procedure assured a steady stream of supplies. Unfortunately, such a base required a guard of approximately an infantry company, perhaps two officers and fifty men, with a similar force needed to escort each wagon train. These demands, of course, seriously handicapped the commander by cutting into the number of effectives available to him.

The snow and bitter cold continued to plague the marching 7th Infantry. The bright sun reflecting off the snow-covered terrain intensified the hardship, and several cases of snow blindness resulted. Nature, as usual, respected neither rank nor profession for both Captain Rawn and Dr. C. H. Hart, Battalion Surgeon, were among the afflicted. Although the weather so moderated on March 20 as to cause the glistening ice to become slushy mud, the senior captain's sight was improved not at all.[26] Ultimately, he relinquished command to the next-in-line, Captain Freeman, and, thus, the journal began.

GEORGE A. SCHNEIDER

---

26. *Bradley*, pp. 141-144 (12-14).

THE FREEMAN JOURNAL

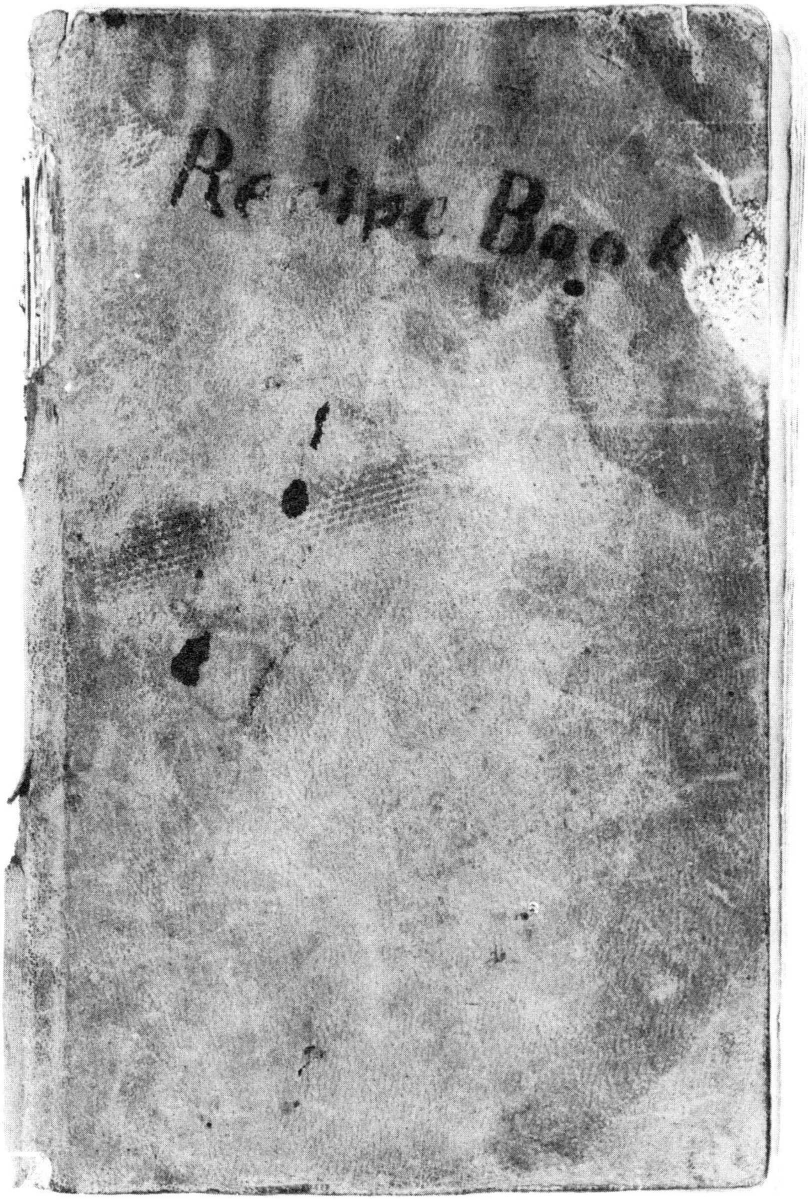

Freeman's journal as it appears today. (*Courtesy of Yale University Library.*)

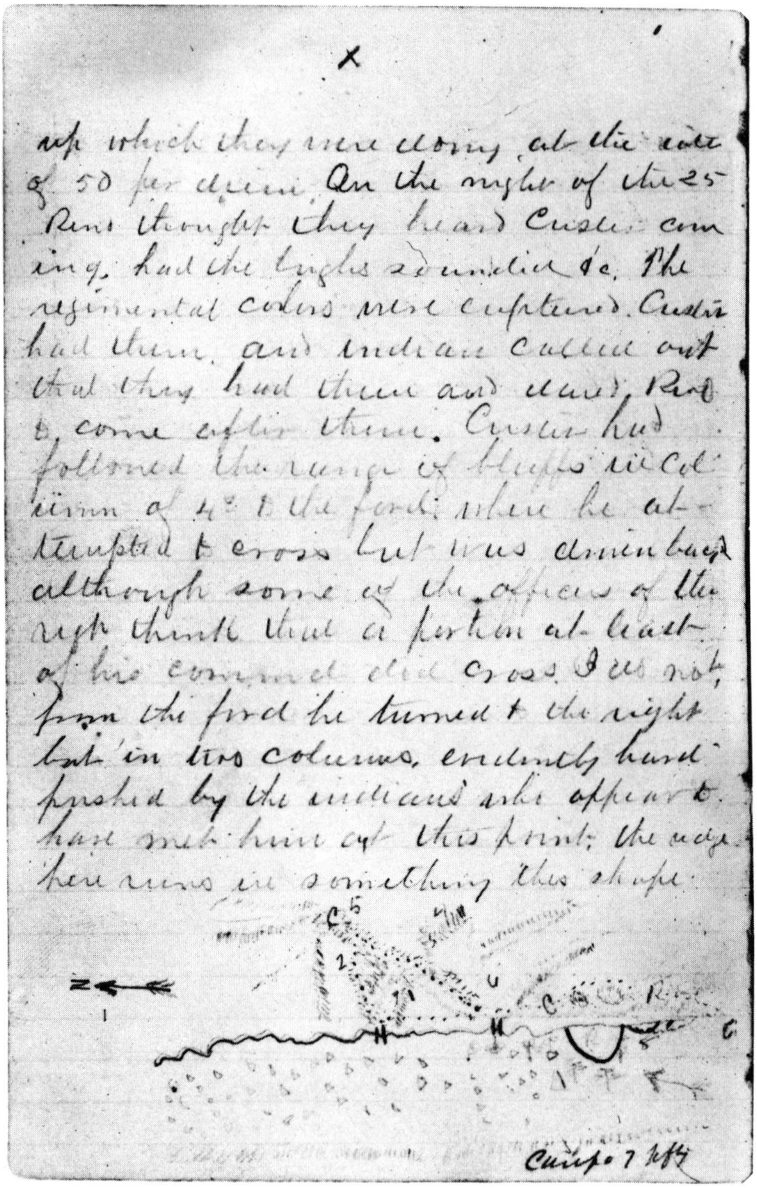

up which they were closing at the rate
of 50 per dozen. On the night of the 25
Reno thought they heard Custer com
ing. had the bugles sounded &c. The
regimental colors were captured. Custer
had them. and indians called out
that they had them and dared Reno
to come after them. Custer had
followed the range of bluffs in col
umn of 4s to the ford where he attempted to cross but was driven back
although some of the officers of the
regt think that a portion at least
of his command did cross. I do not,
from the ford he turned to the right
but in two columns, evidently hard
pushed by the indians who appear to
have met him at this point; the ridge
here runs in something this shape

The journal opened at Freeman's sketch of the Custer Battlefield. (*Courtesy of Yale University Library.*)

March 21. Left Camp at 7AM, marched to Johns[27] and camped, six miles, to allow men to dry clothes and cure feet. Had letter from Sallie.[28] MacCarthy[29] deserted, went toward Helena.

March 22. Left Camp at 7AM, marched to Widow Durgin,[30] 15 miles. Sturgeon and Symes[31] deserted last night. Roads heavy. Camped at 1PM. Went into town, made loan of Corbin, 1¾ quar-

27. A ranch near the head of Little Prickly Pear Canyon, on the old Helena-Fort Benton Stage Road. *Bradley*, p. 145n (15n).

28. Mrs. Freeman. Sarah Darlington and Captain Freeman were married at St. James Church, Zenesville, Ohio, by Rev. John F. Ohl, April 26, 1866. In a letter to General Corbin, dated July 8, 1900, Mrs. Freeman signs herself as "Sallie Darlington Freeman." See *Mss. Freeman Papers, Adjutant General's Office, RG 94, National Archives* (hereafter *Freeman Papers*).

29. Pvt. John McCarty, Co. H, 7th Infantry, had enlisted for five years – all army enlistments of this period were of that duration – at Newport Barracks, Ky., June 5, 1875. *Muster Roll, Co. H, 7th Infantry, January-February, 1876, A.G.O., RG 94, N.A.* (hereafter, *Muster, H, 7th Inf.*). Microfilm provided by N. A.

30. *Bradley*, p. 145 (9, 15) locates the dwelling of the Widow Durgin about four miles south of Helena.

31. Pvt. Henry E. Sturgeon and Charles Symes, both of Co. H, 7th Inf., enlisted at Cleveland, Ohio, on June 12, 1875, and at St. Louis, Mo., on May 1, 1875, respectively. *Muster, H, 7th Inf.*

terly.[32] General [Col. John Gibbon, 7th Inf., a Civil War major general] came in. No letter. He came to the Camp, but I missed him on the road. Dr. Hart[33] put in Sisters' Hospital[34] by Dr. Glick.[35] The two deserters from K Co.[36] released by order of Genl. Gibbon.

March 23. Left Camp at 7AM, marched 18 miles. Camped at Spokane House.[37] Roads very bad. Men with wet feet all day. Reached camp at 2PM. Had some conversation with K about S and J. [not identified] Said Mrs. S was the cause of his [illegible].

March 24. Left Camp at 6:45AM. Camped at Indian Creek at 1:30 PM, marched 19½ mi. Roads good most of the day. [Capt. James M. J.] Sanno [Co. K, 7th Inf.] O.D. [Officer of the Day]. Bolts[38] very drunk last night, fell over tent ropes coming to me for a candle. Sent letters from Rogers [unidentified] to Sallie & J. G. [Gen.

---

32. Strange as it may seem today, Freeman secured a reasonable rate of interest on his loan. At that time Montana was without banking laws, and interest rates varied. Neighboring Dakota fixed the legal rate at 10 percent annually, but any rate not exceeding 2 percent per month might be agreed upon. Jas. H. Dion, "History of Banking in Montana," in *A History of Montana*, (ed. Merrill G. Burlingame and K. Ross Toole) New York, 1957, I, 400, and Jas. S. Foster, *Outlines of History of the Territory of Dakota and Emigrant's Guide . . . of the West*, Yankton, D. T., 1870 (reprint, *South Dakota Historical Collections*, XIV [1928], 169).

33. Dr. C. H. Hart was Acting Asst. Surgeon at Ft. Shaw. *RSW*, 1876, I, 320.

34. St. John the Baptist's Hospital, Helena, was opened on Nov. 1, 1871, by three Sisters of Charity of Leavenworth. Wilfred P. Schoenberg, S.J., *Chronicle of Catholic History of Pacific Northwest, 1743-1960*, Portland, 1962, p. 68.

35. Dr. Jerome or John S. Glick, born Harpers Ferry, Va., 1832, arrived in Montana during the fall of 1862 and at Helena about 1864, became one of Montana's outstanding physicians. He cooperated with the sisters at St. John the Baptist Hospital. Paul C. Phillips and Llewellyn L. Callaway, *Medicine in the Making of Montana* (hereafter, *Medicine*), Missoula, 1962, pp. 82-86, 172, 182, 193.

36. Pvt. Charles Keating and Jas. McFarland of Co. K, 7th Inf., enlisted at St. Louis on June 9, 1875, and March 30, 1875, respectively. Their desertion plans had been stymied by Lieutenant Bradley. *Muster Roll, Co. K, 7th Inf., July-August, 1876, AGO, RG 94, N.A.* (hereafter *Muster, K, 7th Inf.*), and *Bradley*, p. 142 (15).

37. A wayside inn some 22 miles south of Helena. *Bradley*, p. 145 (16).

38. Pvt. Wm. Bolts of Co. H, 7th Infantry, had enlisted at Camp Baker, M.T., June 1, 1872. *Muster, H, 7th Inf.*

Gibbon]. Detached Howard & Wolf[39] at Spokane [House] as escort to Maj [James S.] B[risbin, 2nd Cav.], Fort Ellis.

March 25. Left Camp at 6:40, marched 21 miles. At 2:30 camped at Galen's Ranch.[40] Paid $6.50 for beef for Co. Funny scene with [Lt.] W[oodruff][41] and [Lt.] Bradley[42] last night. Roads from Crow C[reek] heavy.

March 26. Left Camp at 6:30AM, marched one mile beyond Gallatin City. Troops arrived at 1PM. Wagons delayed at ferry, did not arrive until 3PM. Contract train[43] one day's march ahead. Sent forward for rations. Sanno grumbling about roads. Generally disagreeable. Fine day. Gibbon arrived in Camp at 4PM, called at my tent. Appeared satisfied with progress made.

March 27. Left Camp at 6:15, marched 18 miles, camped at Gallatin Bridge at 1PM. Wagons in at 2. Bad roads. J. G. passed at 10AM. [Capt. Wm.] Logan [Co. A, 7th Inf.] and K [probably Capt. Thaddeus S. Kirtland, Co. B, 7th Inf.] went fishing.

March 28. Left Camp at 6:15, marched 17 miles, camped at Ft. Ellis. Roads very bad last half the day. Train an hour behind. Met

---

39. 1st Sgt. George G. Howard and Pvt. Frank Wolf of Co. H, 7th Inf., enlisted at New York City, June 24, 1872, and at St. Louis Aug. 18, 1871, respectively. *Muster, H, 7th Inf.*

40. Was located between Radersburg and Three Forks. Granville Stuart, *Forty Years on the Frontier* (ed. Paul C. Phillips), Glendale, 1957, II, 100.

41. 2nd Lt. Chas. A. Woodruff, Co. K, 7th Inf., battalion adjutant, had temporarily taken over the Mounted Detachment during Bradley's absence seeking deserters. *Muster, K, 7th Inf.*, and *Bradley*, p. 142 (8).

42. 1st Lt. Jas. H. Bradley, Co. B, 7th Inf., had been away from his command after the deserters mentioned in Note 36. His published journal, mentioned elsewhere, is an important reference.

43. John W. Power's wagon train. However that of E. G. Maclay & Co., a "Diamond R" outfit, had taken over the contract and shortly would join the column. *Bradley*, p. 202 (pp. 93, 119). See also "Diary of Matthew Carroll," *Contributions to the Historical Society of Montana*, II (1896), pp. 229-240, and Paul F. Sharp, "Merchant Princes of the Plains," *Montana Magazine of History*, V:1 (Winter, 1955):16.

[Capt. Lewis] Thompson [Co. L, 2nd Cav.] and [Capt. James N.] Wheelan [Co. G, 2nd Cav.]. Dined at Roe's.[44] Mrs. Roe very pleasant and jolly. Genl. G. in ill humor, his arrangements not having met the approval of Dept. Com[mander – Brig. Gen. Alfred H. Terry] as I understand it. Sorry, but hope we will soon get off.

March 29. Lay in Camp. Drew rations for Mess & Co. Had letter from Sallie. Met Brisbin. Dined with Mrs. Worden [wife of 2nd Lt. Chas. Worden, 7th Inf.]. Called on Mrs. Ball, Doane [wives of Capt. Edward Ball, Co. H, 2nd Cav. and of 1st Lt. Gustavus C. Doane, Co. G, 2nd Cav. respectively]. Woodruff appointed Adjt.

March 30. Left Camp about 7:30, marched to foot of big hill, 10½ miles, 11:45. Wagons arrived at 3. Roads execreable, but might be worse. Curran, Copely[45] very drunk.

March 31. Stormy wet. Courier from J. G., telling us to move 2 days farther, to await Contractor's train and make good camp until storm breaks. Wrote to Sallie. 3PM Kirkendall[46] came in, brought mail and letter from Sallie. Contractor's train came up and camped half mile below us.

April 1. Left Camp at 7AM, marched 19 miles, camped at mouth of Shield's River at 1:45PM. Went fishing, caught nothing although others had better success. Received letter from [1st Lt. Levi F.] Burnett [Regimental Adjutant, 7th Inf.], telling me not to wait for

---

44. 2nd Lt. Chas. F. Roe commanded Co. F, 2nd Cav. His account of the expedition appeared as *Custer's Last Battle*, N.Y., 1927.

45. Pvt. Robert Copely and Thos. Curran, Co. H, 7th Inf., enlisted at St. Louis June 7, 1875, and at Boston, June 1, 1874, respectively. Copely had had prior service. *Muster, H, 7th Inf.*

46. Hugh Kirkendall was an early Montana freighter whose name appears often in territorial accounts. See "Commuter's Quandry," reprint from *Montana Post*, Oct. 16, 1868, *Montana, the Magazine of Western History*, IV:3(Summer, 1954):51, and Grace R. Hebard & E. A. Brininstool, *Bozeman Trail*, Glendale, Calif., 1960, I, 227; II, 92.

Contractors as the Cavalry would escort it, to push to the [Crow] Agency fast as condition of things would permit. Road since leaving [Ft.] Ellis full of people going to Black Hills,[47] all well armed and equipped. The woman & men who stopped at [Ft.] Reno in '67[48] lived a year or two at Radersburg, made about $4,000 and went home. Was told by a Mr. Story[49] who carried the mail from [Ft.] K[earney] and was at Reno when the raft upset, came to Montana with those people. Messenger with dispatch to [2nd Lt. Chas. A.] Booth [Co. B, 7th Inf.], announcing arrival of boy at 12 midnight.

April 2. Left Camp 6:15. Men wadded stream at Camp. Sent trains by road, took men short route. Made 4 miles on train.[50] Distance marched 13 miles. Camped at old Indian camp on Yellowstone, 2 miles from Hunters Hot Springs.[51] Sanno grumbling about distance. Like him less and less every day. Weather fine. Contract train well up. Roads hilly but good. Trains got in at 1:30PM, two hours behind men. Went fishing, caught no fish. Man came in from Agency.

---

47. Further details concerning this particular Black Hills immigration appear in John G. Bourke, *On the Border with Crook*, N.Y., 1891, pp. 345-346, 382-387, and Stuart's *Forty Years*, II, 36.

48. Freeman was at Ft. Reno with the 27th Inf. in August of 1867. *RSW* 1867, pp. 54, 55. For details of wagon trains passing Ft. Sedgwick, Colo., from February to September, 1867, see *RSW* 1867, pp. 62-64.

49. Freeman probably refers to Nelson Story who was in the Ft. C. F. Smith general area (which included Ft. Reno) during the period referred to. Story, in true pioneer fashion, was a cattleman, freighter, post sutler and licensed Indian trader. Thomas B. Marquis, *Memoirs of a White Crow Indian*, New York, 1928 (hereafter, *Memoirs*), pp. 23, 25, 60-61, 111, 119-120, 295, 300. However *Senate Ex. Doc. 19, 46th Cong., 3d Ses.*, p. 19, has an *Elias* Story as trader to the Crows in 1876, while Will Robinson's "Digest of Indian Commissioner Reports," *South Dakota His. Collections*, XXIX, Bismarck, 1958, pp. 329, 519 indicate a *Nathan* Story held that post in 1873.

50. *Bradley*, p. 153 (30-31) lauds Freeman for taking the short route.

51. Located about twenty miles east of Livingston. Dr. Andrew J. Hunter recognized its possibilities in 1864, claiming squatter's rights he built a log cabin on the site in 1870. He later erected a large hotel and bath houses to treat patients suffering from rheumatism and similar diseases. *Medicine*, pp. 120, 179, 181. Lieutenant Doane, 2nd Cav., was a son-in-law of Dr. Hunter, see Merrill G. Burlingame, "The Andrew Jackson Hunter Family-Mary Hunter Doane," *The Montana Magazine of History*, I:1(Jan., 1951):8.

[Capt. Walter] Clifford [Co. E, 7th Inf.] got in to the Agency last night. We will make better time if roads do not get worse.

April 3. Left Camp at 6:15AM, marched 16 miles, camped on Boulder at 12. Passed ranch 2 miles from last camp. Saw our Yellowstone guide[52] work. Crossed river 8 mi. out. Ferried all the men in 20 minutes. Crossed the Boulder and camped. Worse stream than the Yellowstone. Made Corral, etc. tonight. Had picket out. Violent snowstorm from about 10:30. Very wet but grew cold and sleety before night. Rivers[53] found Navy revolver; Bolts, a knife, probably relic of some unfortunate hunter. This stream is well named the Boulder for a worse one I never saw. Looking up the stream it presents the appearance of a series of terraces formed by the washing of the rocks and gravel.

April 4. Left Camp at 7AM, marched 8 miles, camped at Deer Creek at 11AM. High wind. Cold snow drifting. Worst day since leaving home. Made short march for that reason. Passed more Blackhillers. Met two of their horses and thought we had made a prize but was mistaken as a party was camped close by. Courier came in with letter and orders to go to Countryman's[54] on the Yellowstone. Cold but clear. Crost [sic] the Yellowstone again.

April 5. Left Camp at 6:15AM, marched 14 mi., camped on Yellowstone. Beautiful valley. Finest I have seen in Montana. Had splen-

---

52. H. M. "Muggins" Taylor was described as "not familiar with the trail along Tullock's Fork, or with the country between it and the Big Horn . . . a good and brave man, who had long lived near the Indian frontier . . . in no sense an experienced plainsman." Edward J. McClernand, "With the Indian and Buffalo in Montana," *Cavalry Journal*, XXXVI (Jan., 1927) (hereafter, *McClernand*):8.

53. Pvt. George Rivers reenlisted at Camp Baker, M.T., July 26, 1875. *Muster, H, 7th Inf.*

54. Horace Countryman had a store at the mouth of the Stillwater, near present-day Columbus, as close as he could to the Crow Agency and yet be off the reservation. His principal commodity was whiskey, and his customers, as can be imagined, Crow Indians. *Bradley*, p. 157 (38); Mark H. Brown, "Muddled Men Have Muddied the Yellowstone's True Color," *Montana, the Magazine of Western History*, XI:1(Winter, 1961) (hereafter, *Brown*):37.

Col. Henry B. Freeman, about 1900. (From: *Companions of the Military Order of the Loyal Legion of the U.S.*, New York, L. R. Hamersly Co., 1901.) (*Courtesy of New York Public Library.*)

did camp. Wood, grass & plenty of fish. Begin to think our worst troubles are over if the promised fording of the Yellowstone proves good as represented. Passed 100 men enroute for B. H. We passed near Bridgers Creek a bluff of the finest conglomerate I have ever seen.

April 6. Left Camp at 6:10. Continued march down Yellowstone Valley. Marched 7 miles and crossed to N. bank. Bad ford, very rocky bottom. Broke axel in contractor's wagon and nearly drowned a mule.[55] Marched 4 mi. after crossing river, had a fine camp. Caught plenty of fish. Sent out hunting party which killed one elk and reported plenty of deer. The latter very wild. Weather fine, cold in the morning but warm after 10AM. Rough country on both sides [of] the river, running from bluff to bluff, leaving in some places barely room for a wagon road. Valley from one to two mi. in width. No chance to send letter.

April 7. Lay in camp all day. Poor fishing, although a great many were caught. The Engineer sergt.[56] while taking observations saw two Indians, supposed to be Crows. Genl came in about 4PM, goes to the Agency tomorrow. Cavalry did not get up.

April 9th (*sic.* Should be 8th.) At about 10AM the Cavalry under Capt. Ball came in and camped some two miles below and soon after Gen'l G, B [risbin], Burnett and myself started for the Agency where we arrived at 3PM and were met by Mr. Clapp,[57] the agent, with a great deal of apparent cordiality although I am told he dislikes ex-

---

55. However *Bradley*, p. 156 (35), says "without difficulty," and English makes no mention of any trouble at the crossing.

56. Sgt. Charles Becker and two privates, Co. D, Engineer Battalion, constituted an engineer party for the "Montana Column," Report of 1st Lt. Edward Maguire, *Report of the Chief of Engineers,* 1876, Washington, 1876, Part III, Appendix 00, p. 699 and map p. 702.

57. Like so many facets of the Custer battle, the administration of Dexter E. Clapp was the matter of considerable controversy. Born in upstate New York in 1830 and ordained a Methodist-Episcopal minister, he forsook the cloth in 1862 to accept a commission with the

ceedingly to have the military about – every agent regarding officers as their natural enemies. Be this as it may, he was very polite to us. Found Capt. C and Lieut. [George S.] Y[oung, Co. E, 7th Inf.] comfortably installed in the agent's house.

April 9th, Sunday. After considerable parley, the Gen'l succeeded in getting a few of the chiefs together for a war talk. Made them a speech. Told them what he was going to do, that the white man went through the country with his head down, saw nothing, etc., that he wanted 25 of their young men to go with him to be his eyes and bring him news, and more to the same effect. After some deliberation, the Indians replied thru Blackfoot, Iron Bull, Old Crow,[58] and one or two other lesser chiefs that the whites & Indians had different methods of warfare, that neither understood the other's method, that their hearts were good to the whites, but they had better remain separate and make war their own several ways, declining to go. The Gen'l was somewhat disappointed and wanted to hear from some of the fighting men of the camp but met no response. I left and soon after the council broke up without any conclusion

---

148th N.Y. Volunteer Infantry. At war's end he was brevetted a brigadier general. Clapp administered the Crow Agency from December 7, 1874, to October 21, 1876. His annual report of 1875 ridiculed the army's efforts to protect the settlements and Federal property. *Report of the Secretary of the Interior, 1875*, Washington, 1876, p. 805. But there were repeated instances of mismanagement on his part and the agency accounts revealed a shortage of $54, 820.79, along with a callous disregard of his own Indian Department regulations. *Senate Ex. Doc. 19, 46th Cong., 3rd Sess.* On August 17, 1877, less than a year after Clapp's departure, George W. Frost, then the agent, found existing records "meager, and in many instances, I regret to say, wholly unreliable, at least so far as relates to statistics." *Report of the Secretary of the Interior, 1877*, Washington, p. 528. On the other hand, LeForge, who served at the Agency during Clapp's tenure, found him honest and capable. *Memoirs*, pp. 106, 111. Clapp later migrated to Kansas, to become a member of that state's House of Representatives from 1878 to his death in 1882. *Yates Center News*, Yates Center, Kans., Friday, June 23, 1882; *National Cyclopaedia of Amer. Biography*, New York, 1907, V:526; and *Heitman*, I:302.

58. Blackfoot was a Crow chief regarded as principal orator of his people. Old Crow was "the greatest chief of the Crows." Grace Raymond Hebard and E. A. Brininstool, *Bozeman Trail*, Cleveland, 1922, I, 156. Iron Bull was recognized for a time as head chief of the Crows by the Federal government. W. P. Clark, *Indian Sign Language*, Philadelphia, 1885, pp. 134-135.

having been arrived at. In the afternoon a dance to celebrate the stealing of a squaw by one of the bands of young men from another band came off on the parade ground of the Agency. In the evening the General was informed that the young men were holding a council, and that a number had decided to go. Divine Service was announced by the Agent and invitations to attend given us. We decided to visit Mrs. Crane-in-the-Skies, a belle of the village.[59] Found her a rather pretty girl. She took quite a fancy to the Gen., exhibited her wardrobe to him. I went from there to Iron Bull's Lodge, and home to bed.

April 10. This morning the recruits assembled for inspection and muster, Bradley in command. 19 were enlisted; the others being absent after their horses. Clifford left for the Camp yesterday P.M. Brisbin and I came down this PM. I found our people had a high disgust at Capt. Ball for leaving them standing about without instructions where to camp yesterday evening. It rained day before yesterday. Cloudy & cold at the Agency yesterday but clear & warm here. Tonight snowing & raining here. Mail goes out tomorrow AM. [1st Lt. Samuel T.] Hamilton [Co. L, 2nd Cav.] came in last night with letter Apr. 2d [*sic*].

April 11. Lay in Camp all day. Clear, snow, cold, generally disagreeable. Gen'l G to come in at 4PM. Train arrived from Agency at dark. Trouble about Off[icer of] Day details with Cavalry. Brisbin sent * * *

> *A blank occurs in Freeman's narrative here; a leaf is missing. However, Lieutenant English[60] was with the regiment, and his account reveals that the main body continued down the Yellowstone, camping some eight miles below Country-*

---

59. *Bradley*, p. 158 (40) identifies her husband as a Crow leader.

60. The manuscript journal of 1st Lt. Wm. H. English (hereafter, *English*), who commanded Co. I, 7th Inf., is also in the Coe Collection at Yale. A transcript copy, provided by that institution, proved helpful in the editing of the Freeman journal.

man's new ranch on the ninth and remained until the thirteenth when a "slow, tedious march" began which brought the regiment to a point just below Baker's Battle Ground[61] *on the fifteenth. The manuscript resumes:*

April 16. Left Camp at 9:40, marched 3 mi. and crossed Yellowstone River. Water quite deep but not a bad ford a little above the riffle. [2nd] Lt. [Chas. B.] Schofield's [Co. L, 2nd Cav.] horse fell and was carried down the river. Lt. nearly drowned, was under the water sometime but, although almost unconscious, held the reins and was pulled ashore. Yesterday the remains of Williams, late a soldier in the 2d Cav. who was drowned last summer, were found in the bushes about 6 miles above BBG by one of the scouts. After leaving River marched 3½ miles to Pryors Creek which is very like the Powder River. Had hard work to cross and camped at mouth at 5PM, marched 7 miles. Crossed river to cut-off bend, the river turning almost due north from Camp of last night, but am afraid we will not gain much in time as the roads are very heavy.

April 17. Left Camp at 8:30, marched 8 miles and halted for water on Arrow Creek. Left at 1PM and camped at Pompeys Pillar at 4½, marched 15 miles. Indians report buffalo moving north with many calves and think this may indi [*sic*] Indians behind them. No signs of any however were seen. Went up on P.P. with Capt. Clifford. Had a beautiful view of the country west, up the valley and toward old [Ft.] C. F. S[mith].[62] The view down the river was cut off about 5 miles distant by a high bluff on the left bank. 31 days out tonight and have marched since leaving Shaw 360 miles. Indians brought in

---

61. Baker's Battle Ground, near Pryor's Forks, was the scene of an Indian attack upon the Northern Pacific Railway Survey and its 2nd Cavalry escort, led by Major E. M. Baker, August 14, 1872. *RSW* 1872, p. 40; *Bradley*, p. 167 (55-63).

62. This post, abandoned in 1868, stood on the Big Horn some fifteen miles south of today's St. Xavier, Mont. *Bradley*, p. 183 (85-86); *Montana Highways* (map), Helena, 1963. A view from Pompey's Pillar appears in *Brown*, p. 35.

buffalo calf, also made a sweathouse.[63] Bradley distinguished himself by sending our mess an antelope shoulderblade. Had a great mind to send it back to him. Are to lay over here tomorrow & issue rations, etc. Mules nearly played out. Weather very warm.

April 18. Lay in Camp all day. Availed myself of the opportunity to bathe and write letters home. Courier left this eve after dark, two of them but a ride before them I would not care to take. High wind, heaps of dust, and unpleasant generally.

April 19. Left Camp at 7AM, marched 19 miles. Train and cavalry crossed river twice. Infty kept on south bank all day. Camped at 3:30, two miles above Stanley's battle ground of '73.[64] High wind all day and rather cold. Sage brush, sand and alkali.

Apr. 20. Left Camp at 7:20. Marched to Bottom on left bank, 2 mi. above Fort Pease.[65] Camped at 4:30PM, distance marched 17 miles. Crossed river at second attempt. Found the place too deep and returned ½ mile up the river. Good ford but deep, villaneous country on this side, very rough and sandy. Bad Camp tonight, high bluffs within easy range, ford or easy crossing in front and brush on two sides of us. Report of large trail on river in the [illegible] tonight. Showed us two pony tracks. Woodruff on rampage 3d time.

---

63. A practice common with most tribes (also in many parts of Europe) not only to combat disease but also as a religious rite. It was perhaps the Indians' greatest hygienic custom to counteract his normal uncleanliness. W. P. Clark's *Indian Sign Language*, Philadelphia, 1885, pp. 364-368; *Medicine*, p. 11; *Memoirs*, pp. 78-79.

64. Scene of engagement opposite mouth of the Big Horn on August 11, 1873, between the Sioux and Custer's eight troops, plus Indian scouts, forming part of the Northern Pacific Railway Survey escort under Gen. David S. Stanley. D. S . Stanley, *Personal Memoirs*, Cambridge, 1917 (hereafter, *Stanley*), pp. 250-251.

65. A stockade erected of rough cottonwood logs, about 75 ft. sq., with a bastion on the northeast and southeast corners. It was located on the Yellowstone, some three miles below the mouth of the Big Horn, and was intended as a trading post. *McClernand*, p. 10; Clyde McLemore, "Ft. Pease, The First Attempted Settlement in Yellowstone Valley," *The Montana Magazine of History*, II:1(Jan., 1952):19; *Bradley*, p. 174 (68).

April 21st. Left Camp at 12M and marched down to Fort Pease, 2 mi. Camped with the mouth of corral against the stockade, infantry on both flanks, cavalry at the out end of corral. A good deal of property was left in the fort, hides, carcasses, coal oil. The flag was and is still flying. Will Logan[66] came in this A.M. with dispatches and mail. No letter for me. Two couriers who left 18 hours ahead of L with large mail have not come in. Four Crows are going out tonight to look for them. Four couriers also leave, two to stop at Baker battle ground, the other two to keep on to Logan's Camp and return. Those to be relieved by the two at B.G. and then return to Logan. I am afraid we'll lost our stock if not careful.

22d. Lay in Camp all day, unloading train. H Co. detailed to escort train to Logan's Camp and return.[67] Detachments to be made to escort train to Ellis and return.

Apl. 23. Left Camp at 6:30AM with H Co. & 6 cavalrymen of Ball's Co. Nooned at crossing of river and then took trail thru the hills on north bank. Very rough road. Watered mules at 4PM and drove to high prairie. Filled kegs at river and made dry camp, poor grass. Had shots at deer but missed. Ambulance & Indians came out after sick Indian, found him & took him back at noon. Big smoke on the creek opposite P. Pillar.

April 24. [Freeman has written over the dates from April 24 to 27 inclusive, correcting them.] Left Camp at 6AM, marched 22 mi., camped on Yellowstone opposite P. Pillar at 2PM. Left the Stanley trail[68] 15 miles back and struck it again 2 miles from Camp. Intended

---

66. Son of the commander of Co. A, 7th Inf., Capt. Wm. Logan. *Bradley*, p. 173 (68).

67; "Logan's Camp" was a temporary depot established at the site of the April 9 stay – on the Yellowstone some eight miles below Countryman's new ranch. It was so named because Captain Logan remained behind with his company to guard these stores. *Bradley*, p. 164 (50); *English*, entries of April 9 and 13.

68. Route of General Stanley while escorting the Northern Pacific Railway Survey of 1873. He moved west from Ft. Rice, Dakota Territory, via Heart River and its great bend, the

to make 5 mi. farther but mules were used up. No signs of Indians yesterday or today, except the smoke in the mountain which is still raising S.E. from P.P.

April 25. Left Camp at 6AM, marched 25 miles and camped 3 miles below mouth of Pryors Creek. No water until camp. Saw two elk on other side of river. Will be obliged to make new road for loaded train.

Apl. 26. Marched to near mouth of Cannon Creek, about 25 miles. Met mail carriers with one letter. Saw 5 elk crossing the river. Had goose liver for supper.

Apl. 27. Left Camp at 6AM, marched about 22 miles and camped on river about 2 mi. above our down camp. Killed elk in foot hills. Logan & Mitch B[69] went to Camp.

April 28. Left Camp at 6AM, marched 8 miles to Logan's Camp. Spent bal. of day in repairing wagons and arranging train. Made detail of [2nd] Lt. [Frederick M. H.] Kendrick [Co. H, 7th Inf.], Sergt. Stein, Corpl. Ruddin,[70] 8 privates to return to Ellis. Dined with Logan on roast goose. Fine dinner.

Apl. 29. Loaded wagons and left Camp at 1PM, marched 6 mi. Found Qr. Mr. statement of stores to be moved 16,000 under the

---

Little Missouri, Glendive Creek, and established the Stanley Stockade on the Yellowstone, following up the left bank of that stream, with a detour around the bluffs (Bad Lands) opposite the mouth of the Powder, then turning northwestward in the vicinity of Pompey's Pillar to Musselshell River, down that stream some 65 miles to its great bend, thence due east to the middle branch of Great Porcupine, to the Yellowstone at the mouth of the Little Porcupine. *Stanley*, pp. 245-254.

69. Edgar I. Stewart, *Custer's Luck*, Norman, 1955 (hereafter, *Stewart*), pp. 104-105, describes Minton or "Mitch" Bouyer as the best scout in the country. *Memoirs*, p. 249; *Bradley*, p. 214 (143-144).

70. Other than Captain Freeman, Lieutenant Kendrick was the sole officer present with Co. H at that time. 1st Lt. Wm. H. Nelson was absent sick. Sgt. George Stein and Cpl.

Mrs. Henry B. Freeman, "the Sallie" of the journal. (*Courtesy of Mrs. Robert D. Carey, daughter of Capt. and Mrs. Henry B. Freeman.*)

amount and requiring four more wagons than estimated for. Mail came in with letter. Kendrick left for Ellis at 12M.

April 30. Left Camp at 6AM. Halted from 11 to 1PM. Marched 15 mi. Met party of Crows who left us at P. Pillar. They report going to Powder River and seeing no sign of Sioux. Crow camp moving down to hunt buffalo which are reported moving north in large numbers. Mustered[71] the Command.

May 1st. Left Camp at 6AM, marched 16 mi., camped on creek 2 mi. from BBG. Mitch Boyer not yet in. Met balance of Crow war party. They have been nearly to Powder river. Say there are no Sioux in the country. Weather very warm. Light shower yesterday, and a little rain during night. [1st Lt. Chas. A.] Coolidge [Co. A, 7th Inf.] Officer of the Day. First snake seen on the trip killed today by a teamster, had 5 rattles. Mail carriers left us tonight for Pease.

May 2. Left Camp at 6AM, marched 12 mi. Camp at coulee next below Pryors Creek. Roads heavy. Camped to rest and get good starts over sand hills to Pompeys Pillar. Weather very warm. River rising. High bluff commanding country for many miles from camp. No game. Out of fresh meats.

May 3d. Commenced storming last night and has kept it up all day. Sleet with high wind, too bad to move in AM. Lightened up a little at 3PM. Hitched up and crossed coulee about half-a-mile, took over

---

Patrick Ruddin enlisted at New York City, May 29, 1872, and at St. Louis, May 20, 1875, respectively. Ruddin had had prior service. *Muster, H, 7th Inf.*

71. Troops were required to be mustered for pay on the last day of February, April, June, August, October and December. *Revised U.S. Army Regulations of 1861, Revised to June 25, 1863* (hereafter, *Regulations*), par. 327, p. 49. New regulations had been drafted in 1876 but were yet to be promulgated. G. Norman Lieber, *Remarks on the Army Regulations*, Washington, 1898, pp. 67-78. Incidentally, muster was rarely followed by pay on the frontier.

two hours. Williamson,[72] mail carrier, with pack mule and two soldiers came up. Sent letter to Sallie. Our own courier tried to cross the river and had to put back, was only at Pompeys Pillar this AM.

May 4. Left Camp at 9AM, marched 17 mi., made dry camp in sight of river. Had we started off [at] the usual hour could have camped on it. Four antelope killed today. first First [*sic*] sign of Indians seen today. Weather cold and cloudy.

May 5. Left Camp at 5AM. Had breakfast at P.P. Left there at 1PM. Camped at 6:12 on dry creek first below P. No grass, no water, very bad camp. Had toothache nearly all day. Off[icer of] Day. Place full of wood ticks. Nasty camp. Long march tomorrow to water, 10 mi.

May 6. Left Camp at 5AM. Had to make road and double teams in camp. Pulled up long hill to Stanley road. Found water in head of coulee tonight. Enough for stock and to spare. Hailstorm at 12, one hour. Terrible toothache for the past three days. Suffered horribly. Marched 18 mi. Camped at mouth of creek. Poor grass.

May 7. Left Camp at 6:30. Doubled teams on hill. Marched 12 miles through bad lands and camped on Yellowstone 8 miles from Pease. Fine camp. Good grass.

May 8. Left Camp at 6AM. Made Fort Pease at 11AM, 8 mi.

May 9. Lay in Camp. Bradley returned from scout.

May 10. Left Camp at 8:30AM, marched 16 miles and camped on Yellowstone. Had cold rain and heavy roads all the PM. Got into camp after dark. Sioux, one seen on other side of river. Found two

---

72. Williamson was a citizen-courier. *Bradley*, p. 206 (126).

of the Indian ponies stolen by Sioux from Pease on the 8th inst. River appears to be making new channel here. Clifford with boats[73] came in at dark, wet and tired, as all of us were. Found a great many petrified fish along the bank of the river.

May 11. Lay in Camp. Fine day. Indians within 500 yds. of Camp last night, prowling about.

May 12. Left Camp at 7AM, marched 5 mi. down bottom and took to hills. Good road. Marched 19 mi. Had fine camp and saw the first buffalo. Taylor, the scout, goes out tonight, up the Rosebud. We stay here until he returns.

May 13. Lay in Camp. Very warm. Scouts returned about 4PM. No Indians. Dispute between them as to whether they had been to Rosebud or not. Bostwick[74] says somebody was afraid to go any farther, meaning Taylor I suppose.

Sunday, May 14. Left Camp at 8AM, marched nearly 17 mi. & camped on river at 5PM. Came down bottom 9 mi., crossed Great Porcupine. Found spring of delicious water at foot of bluffs, Castle Butte. Crossed plateau 2 mi. and came down bad coulee to River bottom. Clifford's Co. killed some buffalo; Bradley too. Soon after camping, furious wind, rain and hail storm came up, upset several tents, [1st Lt. Wm. H.] English [Co. I, 7th Inf.] and Brisbin among the no. Flooded all the rest and is now, 8PM, still raining. Bad night for all hands, especially so for the pickets. Do not move tomorrow. Couldn't if we wanted to, as the bottom is a lake.

---

73. Several boats found abandoned at Ft. Pease were turned over to Captain Clifford who formed a sort of "amphibious wing" of the Gibbon force. *Bradley*, p. 188 (93-94); *Memoirs,* p. 218-219.

74. Henry S. Bostwick was post guide at Ft. Shaw. John Gibbon, "Hunting Sitting Bull," *American Catholic Quarterly Review* II (Sept. 1877) (hereafter, *Gibbon*), p. 673.

May 15. Lay in Camp. Cloudy, cold. No chance to dry clothing, blankets, &c. Bradley with scouts left at dark to find village. The Indians having come in with a report that there is a village on Tongue River, 30 mi. from here. Hall and Rice of H Co.[75] went with him.

May 16. Lay in Camp. No news. Ball went out and killed six buffalo. Dry and sunny. Everybody busy drying blankets and clothes. Don't feel well, ate too much grease lately.

May 17. Alarm last night. Picket at boats saw signals, fired several shots. Companies turned out promptly, but nothing further. Stood out about 1 hour and went to bed and slept quietly until morning. Bradley came in at daylight, reports village on Tongue River. All the Cavalry and 5 Cos. of Infantry go out this PM. K Co. remains in Camp. Hope we will all have good luck. After trying to cross the Cavalry from 9AM until 5PM & only getting one company (Ball's) across in that time and drowning 5 horses, all the rest stampeding, two or three times, the General gave up the idea of crossing the river and is, I believe, intending to move on down this side. Sioux are reported to have been seen on the other side within a few miles, running buffalo, and a number of shots have been heard, although none of them this far have been seen from the Camp. I shall be very much surprised if they do not pay us a visit in fully strong force before long.

May 18. Another alarm last night or, in fact, two of them. The first from the picket at the boat. The Cos. all turned out and just as they were coming in, another alarm was caused by Bradley who was out with two men with a lantern hunting stray horses.

---

75. Pvt. Elijah Hall and Henry Rice enlisted at St. Louis, June 3, 1875, and at New York City, July 2, 1872, respectively. Rice was a member of Bradley's Mounted Detachment. *Bradley*, p. 189 (97); *Muster, H, 7th Inf.*

May 19 [*sic*]. Lay in Camp. Thompson and Wheelan went down the river, to be gone three days, this AM. Bradley started up river this PM for the same time. 4 Indians went across the river to steal horses or take another look for a village. All quiet in Camp last night. Genl's Gibbon and Brisbin both sick.

May 19. Lay in Camp. Bradley returned with mail. Five letters from Sallie. Good! Wish there were more.

May 20. Indians came in this AM with report that large body of hostiles were crossing below us. We are out after them with 3 days' rations, 10 wagons, 150 R[ounds] Ammunition per man. Moved out at 10:30AM, went down 2 mi. below mouth of Rosebud. Saw no signs of Indians. Camped in beautiful place, and Gen'l G talks of sending back for Kirtland (who staid in Camp) and the train.

May 21, Sunday. [1st Lt. Joshua W.] Jacobs [Regimental Quartermaster, 7th Inf.] went back for the train & troops this AM and came in about 3PM. Thompson & Wheelan arrived from below at the same time, and Clifford came in with the boats. He found an Indian grave at the mouth of Rosebud and took some things away, among others a letter from a white woman[76] who is held captive in the Camp, and a letter from a white man to his wife in Iowa and one from her to him. The man was a soldier in the 6 Iowa Cav.[77] and was probably killed by the Indian on whose corpse the letters were found. On their way down, Thompson saw a party of about 50 Indians, with

---

76. The captive white woman was Fanny Wiggins Kelly, taken by Sioux on Horseshoe Creek, about eighty miles north of Ft. Laramie, on July 12, 1864. She was rescued by friendly Indians and returned to Ft. Sully, S. D. December 9, 1864. Her experiences in captivity were initially published as *Narrative of My Captivity Among the Sioux*, Cincinnati, 1871, with other editions following. *Bradley*, p. 198 (113); *South Dakota Historical Collections*, IV (Bismarck, 1908), pp. 109-117; Wright Howes, *U.S. Iana*, New York, 1962, pp. 312-313.

77. The 6th Iowa Cavalry was with Sully Expeditions in the Sioux Wars of 1863-1866. Robert Hugh Jones, *Civil War in the Northwest*, Norman, 1960, p. 67.

the same no. of led horses, come into the bottom on the other side & soon after left, leaving the led horses. Boyer & Hairy Moccasins and another Crow swam the river to steal the horses but they could not find cover nearer than 300 yards so they broke for the herd which was guarded by 3 Indians who saw them when they broke cover and being mounted, drove the herd off before they could get to it. They report seeing a large party moving up the river toward Rosebud, the same probably reported by the Indians on the 20 as moving there on the 19th. They, T. & W., went to Tongue River but saw no more Indians. Rivers caught 3 catfish this evening.

May 22, Monday. Nothing occurred since my last entry. The night passed off quietly. This AM a hunting party from the Cavalry were fired upon by a small party of hostiles. Wheelan's Co. and the Mounted Detcht., under Bradley, went out. Wheelan found their trail and a place on the hill from whence they had been watching the Camp. Saw no Indians on this but a number on the other side of the river. There is undoubtedly a camp on either Tongue River or Rosebud, perhaps on both. B saw nothing. Sergt. Hill[78] crossed river this AM and killed two buffalo and one white tail. One buffalo had an arrow in his shoulder and two or three balls in his body. English with I Co. detailed to go back to meet Supply train. Wrote long letter to wife. Got arbor over tent, &c. Fine day. Went on as O.D.; Booth, O[fficer of the] G[uard], was late. Wheelan volunteered to cross his Co. of Cavalry in an hour tomorrow AM. It is said tonight that he is going over.

May 23, Tuesday. English and Roe left this AM at 7:30. About that time shots were heard on the bluffs, and in a few moments it transpired that two cavalrymen on Ball's Co. H[79] and a citizen teamster

---

78. Sgt. Charles R. Hill enlisted at Dubuque, Iowa, June 28, 1872. *Muster, H, 7th Inf.*

79. The two soldiers were Pvt. Henry Rahmeir, with over ten years service, and Augustine Stoeker, enlisted at Ft. Ellis, December 1, 1871, and at New York City, July 31, 1873, respectively. *Bradley*, p. 202 (119) gives these names as Rahmeyer and Stoker, but Barry

named Quinn had gone out hunting without permission and attracted by a pony, had been surrounded and killed. Capt. Ball and the Dr.[80] with Cav. escort went out and brought the bodies in, but one was scalped, a soldier. One of them had a butcher knife fixed in either side of the head. The men had been shot from above and at close range. The bodies were filled with bullets. A Crow went across the river and captured a pony that had the appearance of having been recently worked in harness. Thought he might have been stolen from the Black Hillers. Plenty of Indians seen around the bluffs today. Mr. Chestnut[81] came down the river from Bozeman in a boat with vegetables, butter, eggs, &c., arrived here about 6PM. Saw no Indians. He reports buffalo by thousands crossing the river between here and Ft. Pease. He asks 8¢ for potatoes, 1.00 for butter & Eggs. Don't want any at that price. Want eggs bad enough but can't afford it. Had two letters from Sallie. Indians were reported to be crossing the river to this side last night. Would not be surprised if they were to trouble English who ought to be stronger than he is. An additional post was put in front of Genl G Tent tonight as it was thought the Indians might fire upon us from the other side of the river, and the 12 Pdr.[82] was run up to the same

---

C. Johnson (ed.) "Dr. Paulding and His Remarkable Diary," *Sidelights of the Sioux Wars*, London, 1967, p. 53, indicates Rehmeyer and Stoker. The initial spelling is that taken from *Muster Roll, Co. H, 2nd Cavalry, March-April, 1876, A.G.O., RG 94, N.A.*

80. Dr. Holmes Offley Paulding of New York, Asst. Surgeon, Medical Dept., U.S. Army, entered the service November 10, 1874, died May 1, 1883. *Heitman*, p. 776; *Bradley*, p. 164 (50). Publication of the doctor's diary is mentioned in previous note. His letters home appeared as "New Light on the Little Big Horn," *Field Artillery Journal*, XXVI:4(July-Aug., 1936):343-360.

81. *Bradley*, p. 203, (121) states Chestnut was a Bozeman gentleman and merchant.

82. While *Bradley*, p. 164 (50), terms this piece "a twelve-pound Napoleon gun," it may be either the bronze 12-pounder Napoleon gun of some 3,000 pounds weight, or the much lighter mountain howitzer, very much the favorite in the West. Spherical case-shot from either gun contained 1½ pounds of musket balls which could be sent up to 1,250 yards, there to scatter its missiles over the target area. The redmen, as can easily be understood, learned to respect these "wagon guns." Edward S. Farrow's *Military Encyclopedia*, New York, 1885, II:401, 443-446; Carl P. Russell, *Guns on the Early Frontier*, Berkeley & Los Angeles, 1957, p. 263, and Robert A. Murray, "Artillery Against the Northern Plains Indians, 1823-1890," *Gun Report*, XIII:5(Oct., 1967):18-29.

point. Old Show His Face[83] cried when he saw the dead bodies today and gave one of his best blankets to one of them. Sergt. Hill was on the other side of the river and killed a deer this AM, but I think today's work will put an end to small hunting parties.

May 24, Wednesday. In consequence of the report that the Indians were crossing last night, we were all up and out on the picket line at 2:30AM and waited there for daylight. Nothing came of it. Went to bed again until 8. Nothing of interest during the day. No Indians to be seen. Am afraid they may have gone after English. We will know tomorrow evening as Roe is due at that time.

May 25, Thursday. Out at 2:30 again this AM until daylight. Nothing of interest. Very warm day, the first for some time. It appears that Roe is not expected back until tomorrow, if even then. Gen'l G talks of sending message to Gen'l Terry by boat with an officer and ten men. T is expected at Glendive Creek, 130 miles, on the 28th inst.

May 26, Friday. Turned out again this AM. Nothing occurred. Turned in again little after daylight and slept until 8. Was awakened by report that Roe was in sight, and in a few moments he came. Reports leaving English about 10 mi. this side of Fort Pease. Had seen no Indians. A curious thing occurred today at 1PM; the moon was in the Zenith and the sun shining brightly, a star was plainly visible about a degree from her and a little above the line between her and the sun. I never saw or recollect hearing of such a thing before. It was the evening star and accompanied the moon to her setting. Was Officer of the Day.

May 27, Saturday. Nothing unusual last night. Bradley crossed the river with his detacht. this AM on a scout. E Co. also crossed 1PM.

---

83. *Bradley*, p. 203 (121) identifies this Indian as Little Face, of a kindly disposition.

B came in, saying he had seen a big smoke on the Rosebud 18 to 20 miles [*torn*] also a large band of horses, thinks it a village. The Indians must think we are a surveying party otherwise they would hardly remain so near us and watch us as little as to permit a small party like B's to go so near their camp without attacking it. Williamson and two soldiers left in a boat this evening with letters for Gen'l Terry. Ball and Thompson left at same time for mouth of Tongue River.

Sunday, May 28. Genl G with Cavalry escort went out to look for next Camp this AM. 10 Sioux seen on this side river. Mr. McCormick[84] with mail and boatload of vegetables, &c. came in about noon, bringing mail and letters from Sallie, also orders from St. Paul[85] for this command to join Genl T at Glendive Creek at once. All the transportation goes back to meet train. Soon as it comes up, we march down, but I think Terry will he here before the train comes up. There are to be two steamers, one of which will be at the disposal of J. G., as well as a small amount of supplies. Am afraid all our work will be for naught unless the different columns co-operate more intelligently than heretofore. Crook ought to be nearing us by this time. Sanno and Roe, with the train, leave in the AM. Fine shower today. Cooled the AM nicely.

May 29. Sanno with train left this AM. Logan moved over and took his place. Nothing occurred except that Bradley made an ass of himself in Wheelan's tent, at which Logan got himself worked up and wrote B a letter asking whether he had any reference to him in his allusions. Bradley replied by asking L some questions.

---

84. Paulinas W. McCormick was sutler of the "Montana Column" but, also, had been with the Pease Expedition. Clyde McLemore, "Ft. Pease, The First Attempted Settlement in Yellowstone Valley," *The Montana Magazine of History*, II:1(Jan., 1952):19.

85. Headquarters of the Department of Dakota was at St. Paul, Minn. The Department embraced the state of Minnesota and the territories of Montana and Dakota. *RSW* 1876, pp. 42, 439.

Fort Shaw, Montana, 1889. Officers' quarters fronting on south line of parade ground. (*Courtesy of U.S. Signal Corps and National Archives.*)

May. 30. Nothing of interest. Two Indians who went out last night to find the Sioux camp and steal horses, came back and reported having seen 30 Sioux riding down the river. This was after dark. They concluded their medicine was not strong enough. They say the camp has moved to within about ten miles of us. This certainly very strange, if true.

May 31. Nothing of interest today. Wheelan went 17 mi. upstream to reconnoiter, saw nothing.

June 1st. Rained all night. Sleet and snow this AM. This has been a most miserable day. Rain, hail, and snow, a counterpart of this day 5 years ago,[86] except that instead of marching we were [*sic*] lay in our tents today. Nothing of interest occurred.

June 2d, Thursday. High wind this AM. Ground covered with snow, but went off toward noon. Cold and disagreeable all day. Nothing of interest to note. Wish the trains or the steamboat would would [*sic*] come. Am awfully homesick.

June 3d, Friday. Went on the picket line at 2AM. Very cold. Could not get warm again after returning to bed and spent a miserable morning. Heavy frost and nearly ¼ inch of ice. Nothing of interest. Logan detailed to build bridge 1½ miles below Camp. Ball has gone this AM to bridge the Porcupines.

June 4, Saturday. Fine, cool morning. Logan left at 5AM on his bridge building expedition. Capt Sanno with Supply train arrived at 3PM. Got Potatoes, Butter, and Eggs – the latter in not very good

---

86. An apparent reference to the movement of two companies of the 7th Infantry, led by Freeman, from Ft. Shaw on October 20, 1871, to disperse a camp of Canadian half-breeds in which whiskey and arms were illegally being sold to the Indians of the "old Ft. Belknap area." After accomplishing its mission, the column turned homeward but was overtaken by a terrific storm on November 24. Before camp could be made, there was a sudden drop in temperature, together with heavy snowfall and a violent northwest wind. Nearly half of the men suffered frozen hands or feet and ten amputations were necessary. A.B. Johnson, "The 7th Regiment of Infantry," *The Army of the U.S.* (ed. Theo F. Rodenbough & Wm.

condition, having been packed in pine saw-dust which tainted them, more or less, and a good many of them were broken. Start in the AM for Glendive Creek.

June 5, Sat. [*sic*] Left Camp at 10AM. A good deal of talk. About 9 miles and camped near the river on a slough. Nothing of interest.

June 6. Left Camp at 6:50, marched 10½ miles. Pulled up a terrible hill this AM and came to the river, down a creek. Camped on the river.

June 7. Left Camp at 8AM, marched 21½ miles. Good road. Camped on River. Going down tiny coulee.

June 8. Left Camp at 8AM and pulled over the bench to a creek which we followed down about 6 miles. Crossed a low divide and curve to the river. Marched about 12 mi., nooned and drove until 7PM, making a total distance of 18 miles. During the day one of our Indians picked up a sack containing ammunition and rations, and saw the tracks of two shod horses which we suppose were scouts from the Lincoln column.

June 9, Wednesday. Was aroused this AM by an orderly, calling me to the General. Went up and was told that I would be in command as he was going down the river to meet Genl Terry who was coming up on a boat. The long looked for steamer arrived in sight at noon and in an hour later was moored opposite our camp. Genl Terry sent up for all the officers. We went down and were introduced. His Cav. are 20 miles up Powder river and will scout to the Forks and cross from there to Tongue. We go back to the Rosebud. Genl T thinks we will be thru in about 20 days, but says he will stay out all Summer if necessary. He had a letter for me from Rob [unidentified] but left it in his camp. Rained hard nearly all the afternoon.

L. Haskin), New York, 1896, p. 505. Apparently, Mrs. Frances M. A. Roe refers to this incident in her *Army Letters from an Officer's Wife, 1871-1888*, New York, 1909, pp. 210-211.

June 10, Saturday. Lay in Camp all day. This AM the Genl sent for me and told me he had concluded to accept Lt. K pledge to abstain from the use of all intoxicating liquor, &c., while an officer of the 7th Infantry. The Cavalry left for the Rosebud this PM at 2 oclock. Clifford and Kirt were somewhat overcome at the separation.

June 11, Sunday. Left Camp at 6:20, marched 9¾ miles. Made one crossing of Mud Creek, found the other two too deep. Found the Cav. pulling up the bluffs. They were from 5½ to 12:30 pulling up, so we concluded to noon and work the road. Made detail for that purpose but rain coming on, went into Camp and sent 3 Cos. later to make the grades. Showery all the PM. Sun dogs visible. Cold, had fire in tent. Water unfit for use, but fortunately had a little in barrel from the river. Have turned our faces homeward, would be glad if we were not to stop this side of Shaw.

June 12, Mon. The Diamond R train started at 6AM. We all got up the hill just opposite Camp at 9AM. My wagon upset but broke nothing. Found spring of good water to left of road, also water and wood in ravine 6 mi. farther, but came down to river bottom and camped at some wet weather holes. No wood, little and bad water. Camped near the scene of Custer's first fight.[87] Cav. about 12 mi. ahead of us.

June 13. Left Camp at 7AM. Crossed two bad coulees, and in a little rut upset H Co. wagon and broke reach[88] of another. On the road 9 hours. Made about 15 miles and had nice camp at mouth of Coal Creek. Had lunge ¼[89] for supper. Camped on river.

---

87. On August 4, 1873, Custer with eighty-five men had a brush with the Sioux at a point almost opposite the confluence of the Tongue and Yellowstone. *Stanley*, p. 249.

88. The coupling pole which connects the front and rear gear of some wagons. Nick Eggenhofer, *Wagons, Mules & Men: How the Frontier Moved West*, New York, 1961, p. 41.

89. *Lunge* or *longe* – a species of pike. Frederwick W. Hodge, *Handbook of the American Indian, North of Mexico*, New York, 1959, I:815. Mrs. Frances M. A. Roe, *Army Letters*, p. 194, comments on a queer fish called the "ling" which had three sides, was long and slender, but really delicious.

June 14. Left Camp at 7AM and arrived near our old camp 4 miles below Rosebud at 2PM. Marched about 12 miles. Very warm day. Maj. Thompson with 2 Cos. of Cav. leaves in the A.M. for Ft. Pease and will send mail from there. Wrote to Sallie.

June 15. As we are to be in this camp for several days, I took matters very quietly this AM and did not get up until about 8. Had my tent fixed up and nothing to do the balance of the day. I think that when the boat comes up we will cross the river. Thompson and Wheelan left for Pease this AM before I was out of bed.

June 16. Lay in Camp. Very warm. Did not feel well all day. Order to have 3 days cooked rations in readiness when the steamer comes in sight. Suppose we are to cross and go after the village supposed to be on the Rosebud. Crow scouts came in and reported a big smoke on O'Fallon Creek, a small stream about 15 miles above here. They think the soldiers have burned a village there. 4 men came in from Wheelan's Co. with a sick man from the spring 25 miles above.

17. Lay in Camp. Nothing of interest.

18. Lay in Camp. Maj. [Marcus A.] Reno came down the Rosebud with 6 Cos., 7th Cav., expecting to meet boats. Will go to Tongue River to meet him. He came across from Powder. Saw plenty of of [*sic*] old camps but no Indians.

June 19. Wheelan & T came in this evening. Saw nothing. Reno went down to Tongue. The big smoke seen the other day was from his command on Rosebud.

June 20. Still waiting for a boat which ought to have been here before this. H, K, & E Cos. leave in the AM for above to make roads as far as the Great Porcupine, 25 mi. The hottest day we have had.

June 21. Left Camp at 6AM, marched 7¼ miles and made road across dry coulee. Marched 3 mi. and made road across Little Porcupine. Marched 5 miles and camped at spring of deliciously cool water. At Little Porcupine, Indian scouts told me the boat was coming and that Custer was at the Rosebud. Scout Taylor overtook us with confirmatory report. We soon saw the smoke of the steamer. At 5PM, Ball with the rest of the command overtook us and ordered us to move to his camp, 1 mi. further on. Packed up and got in just before dark. At dark hailstorm came up. Herd stampeded, ran out and helped get it in. One stone picked up and measured by Capt. Logan was 2 inches long, 1¾ wide. Capt. Ball was knocked down by one. It fortunately lasted but ten minutes, and we succeeded in getting the herd corralled. Marched 15 miles.

June 22. Left Camp at 6AM, marched 5 miles to Great Porcupine. Very bad road across bottom. Cavalry left us at 5AM, overtook it, went about half-mile above them. Made crossing and passed them. Took the bench up coulee. Ball was very much out of humor at finding us ahead. We allowed him to pass and went into camp on river. Cav. kept on.

June 23. Left Camp at 6AM, marched 1½ miles. Crossed slough 4 mi. to Froze-to-Death Creek, 3 mi. across bench. Found fine water in spring, 9 miles to Pease bottom, 1 mile to slough. Bad crossing 3 miles to slough. Bad crossing 1 mile to Camp on River. Saw smoke of steamer below last night's Camp. Taylor saw 15 Sioux on opposite side.

June 24. Left Camp at 6AM. Steamer passed Camp early this AM and stopped at Fort Pease for wood, and went on to Cavalry Camp, 2 mi. above Pease. Began crossing the Cav. to south bank of river. We came up, crossed and the whole command moved out 5 miles and camped on Tullocks Fork. Genl G remained on boat, sick. Genl Terry in command.

June 25, Sunday. Left Camp at 5AM, moved 2½ miles up Tullock, took to hills and crossed to Big Horn. Marched 19 miles through dry, rough country. Very hot. No water. Men played out when we reached river. Halted 2 hours. Cav. went on to camp 4 mi. Infantry came and found the Cavalry preparing to go on to Little Horn, 5 miles farther. Inf. to come on early in the AM. Crows having brought in word that there was a large village on that stream. Rained all night. Slept sitting against a tree.

June 26. Left Camps [*sic*] at 4:20, marched 15 miles and came up with the Cavalry who were waiting for us. Genl Gibbon had in the meantime joined us from the boat which came in sight before we had left camp. Three of the Crows who had been with Custer had run away and crossed the Big Horn. Our scouts discovered them and learned that Custer had attacked a large village at noon on the 25 and had been whipped, most of his regt. killed, and the remainder corralled in the hills, that Mitch Boyer and three of the Crows had been killed. All our Crows deserted us on learning this, cried, and besought us not to go on; we were certain to be killed, that the whole Sioux nation was there, &c., &c. We pushed on. At dark camped after marching 30 miles. While waiting where we came up to the Cav., Muggins Taylor was sent out to see what he could and report. He came back and reported a large fire up the Little Horn. Genl Gibbon came up and said it was all right, Custer had the village, or the Indians were burning it up themselves. Just before we left this point, Genl Terry offered $200 to anyone who would carry a dispatch to Genl Custer. Taylor and Bostwick started but were fired upon and came back. We nooned from 3 to 5PM on the Little Horn, and soon after we started again. The Indians began [*sic*] show themselves in front and on the bluffs. At one point especially they were in column very much like a Co. of Cavalry; many of the officers thought they were Cavalry. Taylor said he had seen the 7th Cavalry, but their Ree Indians had fired at him so he did not go in. Some columns of Indians made their appearance, and it seemed to be the general opinion that they were cavalry — some said Crook, some Custer, and, finally, that 2 men had been seen to ride up to Roe who was on the bluff and shake hands. I still thought they were Indians and won a cigar. We camped at dark in the middle of the bottoms in two lines, stock & HeadQrs. inside. I slept soundly, tired out.

June 27. Left Camp at 4, Ball's Co. in advance. At this point the stream makes an abrupt turn across from east to west, the banks being heavily timbered and crowding our line of march on the bluffs. A skirmish was sent through the timber, but we had seen the last of Mr. Lo the night before. The village had left. The Indians we had seen were the rear guard and flankers. After 3 miles march we came upon the village, or rather what had been the village. Half a dozen lodges with dead Indians were still standing, while any quantity of poles and a heterogeneous lot of equippage were scattered about, showing that they had moved in great haste. A large number of horses, dead, wounded, and sound, were in sight. The sound ones were picked up. Half a mile farther we came in sight of Maj. Reno's 7th Cos. who were corralled on a high bluff on the east bank, 3 or four miles above us, & about a mile from where the first attack was made. We moved on up. Lt. Bradley, who was on the east bank, sent in to say that he had seen 42 bodies of soldiers, and soon after that he had found 190 in half a mile further up. We found 40 more and quite a number of dead horses. We soon had a scout from Maj. Reno, and the command went into Camp. [1st] Lt. [Donald] McIntosh & [2d Lt. Benjamin H.] Hodgson [7th Cav.] were found close to the camp & buried. Our Dr's went up to Reno to care for the wounded of whom there were 41. The stench from the dead bodies and dead horses was something terrible. The rest of the day was spent in making litters and bringing the wounded into our camp and burying the dead which latter task was not completed at dark. All the bodies except that of Genl Custer were more or less mutilated. All were stripped. Capt. [Myles W.] Keogh had an *Agnus Dei*[90] at-

---

90. *Stewart*, p. 469, advises this medal was actually a *Medaglia di Pro Petri Sede* which had been conferred by Pope Pius IX.

tached to a gold chain about his neck. It was left there. Capt. [George W.] Yates' finger had been cut off to get his ring.

June 28. Horse litters were made today to carry such wounded as were able to ride in that way today. Cavalry sent on the trail of the village which camped 10 miles from us on the 26th for that night and moved off in the AM. The trail appeared to split, some going toward the Canon of Bighorn, some toward Kearney, others up the Little Horn. They have dropped a large amount of stuff in the ravines leading up to the tablelands. We moved out of camp at 6PM; the men carrying 21 wounded on hand litters, the rest on horse litters. It required nearly the whole command to move the wounded 5 miles and took us until after midnight to get to camp.

June 29. We found from last night's experience that it would be impossible to get on carrying the wounded by hand, so today was spent in making horse litters enough to carry all the wounded. The litters were made of two poles 16 feet long ~~two two crossbars at the~~ [*sic*] a crossbar 4 feet from either end, a lacing of rawhide between the bars upon which the wounded were laid. The ends of the long poles in front and rear of the crossbars made shafts into which the mules were put, and sling rope passed over the saddles. Each mule was led by a man on foot while two others walked at either side of the litter to steady it. In this way we marched 14 miles to the boat which we found waiting for us at the mouth of Little Horn, and we got into camp after putting all the wounded on the boat at daylight or 2:30 AM on the 30. As in nearly all night marches, there was more or less confusion. We had to leave the bottom about 4 miles above the mouth and to take to the bluffs; there appeared to be no one who knew the way, and when we got to the bluffs over the boat, everything came to a standstill. It was very dark. We finally found a ravine with a trail leading down, but it was too dark to see where it led. I suggested to Genl Terry that I could take the Infantry and build fires to light it up. He told me to do so. Lewis Thompson and myself followed the trail out, and in a short time we had it lighted up

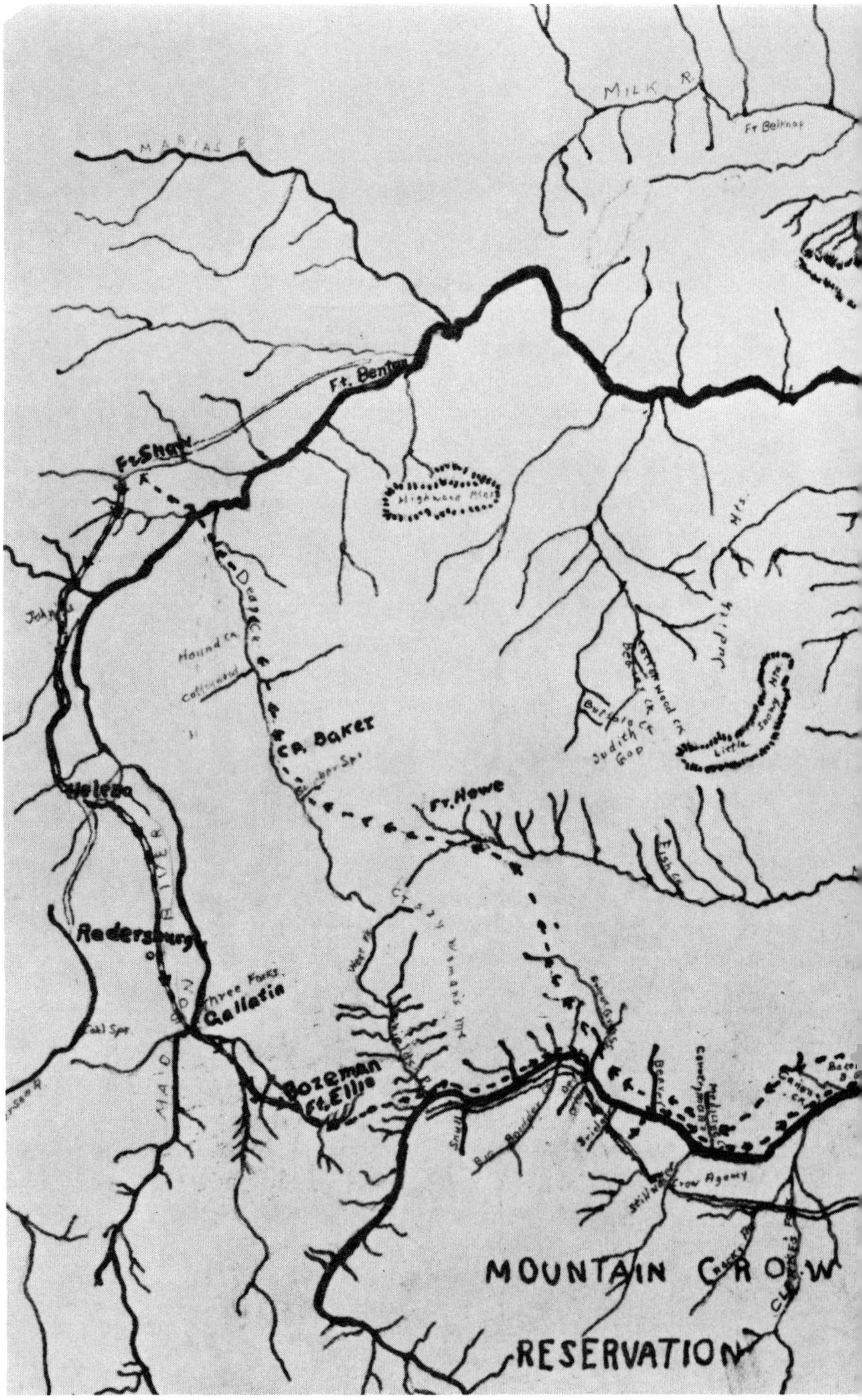

Marches of the 7th Inf. during the Yellowstone Expedition of 1876. Based on the journals of Capt. Henry B. Freeman and 1st Lt. Wm. L. English, 7th Inf., the manuscripts of which are with the Coe Collection at Yale University Library.

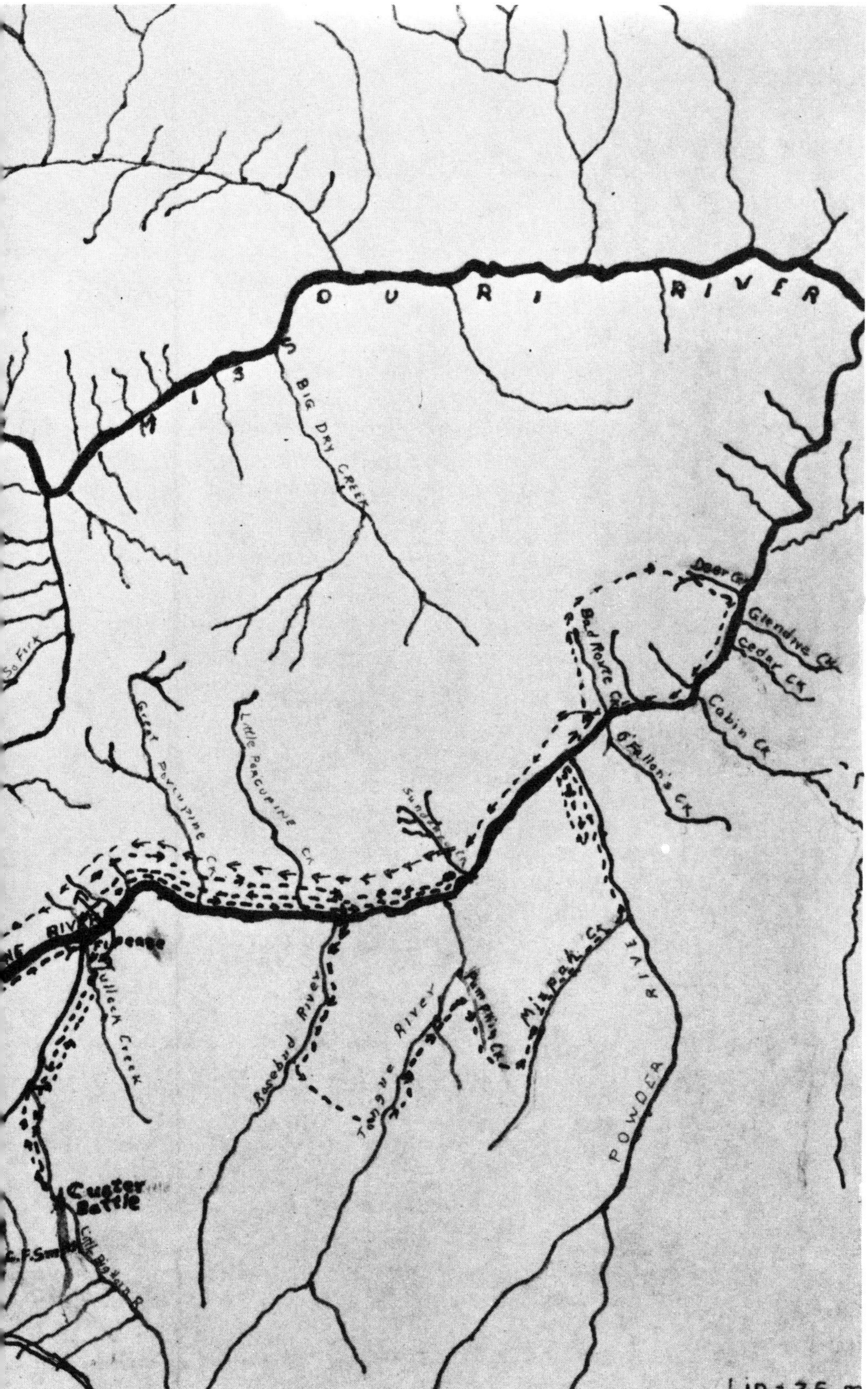

(Marches plotted on map prepared by Lt. Robert H. Fletcher, appearing in *Report of the Secretary of War for 1877*, vol. I.) Location of added sites are approximate only.

and everything on the move. Genl T and staff went on the boat and to bed, also Gibbon. Thus ended our march to and from the battlefield.

Incidents of Custer's March from mouth of Rosebud and the battle.

Genl Custer and his command left the boat at mouth of Rosebud on the 22d of June. Genl Terry offered him the 4 cos. of the 2d Cav. and the battery of 3 Gattling guns, both of which he declined, saying his force was strong enough to whip all the Indians in the Northwest. This opinion was that of most, if not all, the officers of his command. Genl Gibbon said to him: "If you find the Indians in great force, wait until we get up." It having been arranged that we were to meet him at nearly the spot where the battle was fought on the 26, or 7 at latest. We, by dent [*sic*] of the hardest marching I ever made, were on time. Our marches for the next 6 days being never less than 21 and once 30 miles per day, over a terribly rough and broken country. Custer pushed rapidly forward, having excellent ground, making forced marches, and from the morning of the 24th to the time he made the attack had marched 75 miles, and & [*sic*] the fact that his command was worn out was one of the ~~principal~~ [*sic*] causes of his defeat,[91] independent of the overwhelming numbers he encountered and his very faulty arrangements for the attack – for had his men and horses been fresh, he might have been able to withdraw at least a considerable portion of his command. As it was, the Indians had no trouble in running his horses down. On the 24 his scouts reported a very large village; all united in describing it as the largest ever seen. They also reported that the column had been seen for the day past by the Sioux. In fact, a party sent back to the camp of the night be-

---

91. Support for Freeman's contention is found in Elwood L. Nye's "Marching with Custer," *Army Veterinary Bulletin*, XXIV(April, 1941):114-140. (The Nye article was republished under the same title, Glendale, 1964.) Stewart discloses that two privates of Co. C, 7th Cav. dropped out of Custer's battalion as their horses were exhausted. "The Reno Court of Inquiry," *The Montana Magazine of History*, II:3(July, 1952):36. See also Reno Report, *RSW* 1876, p. 479.

fore had found one in the camp and 6 others on the hills around it. He halted two hours and then pushed on. On the morning of the 25th, the scouts reported the village close. Custer rode up to see it. The scouts pointed it out, but he was unable to see it. They again told him it was the largest one they had ever seen. Custer rode back to his command which had been halted, told them of it. Said it was a big village, divided his regt. into 3 battalions: 5 cos. with him, called the center, 3 Co's under Reno, the advance, 3 Cos. under Capt. [Frederick W.] Benteen, one with the pack train. The whole command moved at a gallop down the valley. Soon came to a lodge and traces of fresh camp. They thought the Indians were running, set fire to the lodge, and increased the gait. They soon came in sight of the Indians and the upper end of the village. Benteen with his 3 Co. was ordered to pull out to the left to cut them off from the mountains, Reno ordered to charge straight down the valley. Custer pulled the 5 Cos. out to the right to strike the village lower down, first great mistake, in dividing his force in the face of one largely superior. Reno made his charge but was soon stopped and put upon the defensive. Custer crossed the creek and took to high bluffs from where he must have seen the whole camp, and, also, that by this route it would be next to impossible for him to get to the village and that the ground was next to impracticable for cavalry. Here he should have turned back and joined Reno. This was the last seen or heard of Custer and his 5 Cos. until they were found by us on the ridges and in the ravines three miles below this point and opposite a ford leading into the center of the village. In the meantime, Benteen finding the ground over which he had been sent impracticable, came up after Reno who was surrounded by Indians on all sides ~~and seeing how matters stood~~, ~~joined his force to that of Reno where they fought for some time~~. ~~In the meantime, one co. with the pack-train was coming in and took to the bluff on Custer trail. As they were raising the bluff, they were met by a heavy fire and dismounted and luckily were able to hold down~~. [*sic*] Reno seeing himself with 3 Cos. unable to advance and the Indians closing in upon him, gave orders to mount and cut through the Indians to the bluffs. Up to this time he had lost no men, but now began a stampede in which the Indians closed in, fighting almost hand-to-hand. 46 of his men were killed before they could cross the stream, some of them in the water. After getting on the bluffs, where he was joined by Benteen and the co. with the packs, he attempted to follow after Custer but could not. He then took the position in which he remained, fighting until we came up on the 27. When Reno fell back, Lt. [Chas. C.] DeRudio and several men had their horses killed and were left in the timber. After several narrow escapes most of them got to the command on the night of the 25, after the Indians had left. They could see the squaws mutilating the dead and could see the Indians killed and wounded on the (25 & 6) [*sic*] being carried into the village. On the evening of the 25, the Indians moved the upper part of the village down about 2 miles and settled down again, evidently intending to stay until they had used this up which they were doing at the rate of 50 per diem.[92] On the night of the 25, Reno thought they heard Custer coming, had the bugles sounded, &c. The regimental colors were captured.[93] Custer had them, and Indians called out that they had them and dared Reno to come after them. Custer had followed the range of bluffs in column of 4's to the ford where he attempted to cross but was driven back. Although some of the officers of the regt. think that a portion, at least, of his command did cross, I do not. From the ford, he turned to the right but in two columns, evidently hard pushed by the Indians

---

92. Freeman here seems to refer to the extensive range required to graze the vast Indian pony herds.

93. Freeman is in error here. The standards of mounted units correspond to infantry colors. The post-Civil War cavalry did not have the national colors but only the blue silken regimental standard, 29 x 27 inches, with the U.S. coat of arms embroidered thereon and regimental designation appearing in a scroll beneath the eagle. When operating against hostile Indians, where the element of surprise was generally sought, a bright fluttering flag would, at the very least, neutralize all efforts at concealment. Consequently, such banners were usually kept furled and cased back with the trains when on campaign. This was true at the Little Big Horn, for the cased 7th Cavalry standard was with the packtrain which joined Reno and, hence, was not captured by the Sioux. However, a number of company guidons, similar to the national colors but of smaller size, were lost that day. *Regulations*, par. 1468, p. 462; W. A. Graham, *Custer's Battle Flags*, New York, 1952, p. 5; Melbourne C. Chandler, *Of Garryowen in Glory: The History of the 7th U.S. Cavalry*, Annandale, 1960, p. 406.

who appear to have met him at this point. The ridge here runs in something this shape:

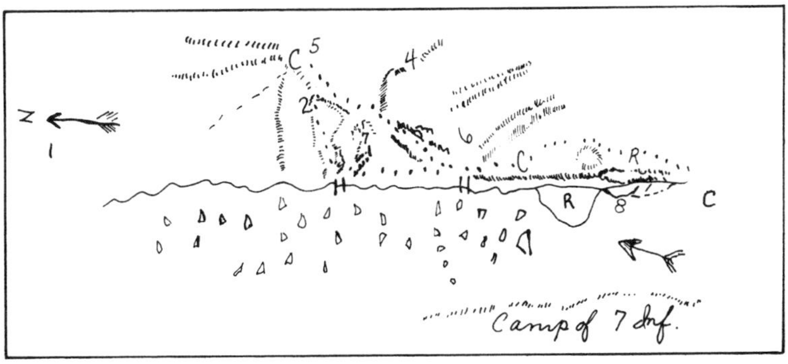

C at upper end is the point where Reno crossed the creek.

The dotted lines along the bluff to the ford, Custer's trail.

At 6 the first bodies were found.

At one 1 [*sic*] & 4 there were indications that they had dismounted and made a stand, and again at 2.

At 5, the highest point on the ridge, Custer was killed with what remained to him of his 5 cos.

From the upper ford || to 5 is about ¾ of a mile; from the same point to the upper C is 3½ miles; from lower R to upper R, by the trail, 2 mi.[94]

The Indians, Crows [*inserted*], say that there were more Sioux killed from Custer's point than in all the rest of the fighting below the ford.

7 is a ravine which toward the upper end is very steep and forms a pocket in which 28 bodies were found.

The total loss was Custer's 5 Cos., 240, 1 [?] Officers; Reno 100, 2 Officers, 1 Asst. Surg., 2 A[cting] A[sst.] Surg. Aggregate 355.[95]

---

94. Maguire's Map of the Custer Battlefield (*Report of the Chief of Engineers*, 1876, Part III, p. 702) and that prepared by the U.S. Geological Survey (*Montana, Custer Battlefield*, Edition of Sept., 1908) reveal that Freeman's "on the spot" estimates were reasonably accurate, except for the initial figures. Here are the comparisons, mileages being approximate:

	Freeman	*Maguire*	*Geo. Survey*
Upper ford to "5"	¾	1¾	1 5/8
Upper ford to Upper "C"	3½	3¼	3¾
"R" to "R"	2	1½	2

95. Like so many elements of the Custer tragedy, even the number of casualities is uncertain. Sherman gives the losses as 12 officers, 247 enlisted men, 5 civilians and 3 Indian scouts

June 30. I met Genl Terry on the boat this AM; he said my suggestion about fires last night was a capital idea. The boat will leave us here. We take the same old road home. Mustered at 3PM and moved Camp to other side of Little Horn.

July 1. Left Camp at 5AM, marched to our old camp on Big Horn.

July 2. Left Camp at 4AM, the 2d Cav. in advance. It was late getting out. Marched 20 miles to Tullocks Fork, rested two hours, and marched 6 miles to river. Ferried across by steamer and went into Camp. Wrote long letter to Sallie, to go via Bismark by boat.

July 3. Boat left this AM for Bismark. Col. [Edward W.] Smith, ADC [on staff of Gen. Terry], goes to make arrangements for new campaign if we are to stay out any longer. Whether we do or not depends upon Genl Crook's success. We have at all events made requisition for clothing, &c., for 2 months. It will take the boat 20 days to make the trip. By that time, we will be heartily sick of this place.

July 4. Sanno left the Mess on the 2d. Good riddance, a more disagreeable man it has never been my lot to encounter. Wrote a letter to Sallie tonight. 2 of the Indians started home tonight; the three that staid with us each have 6 ponies. The Genl wants 150 or 200 of them to join us.

July 5. Went with a number of officers to call on Genl Terry this evening. Had singing and a pleasant time. Went afterwards to the 2d Cav.

---

killed, with 2 officers and 51 enlisted men wounded. *RSW* 1876, p. 35. But there is little concurrence. See *Bradley*, pp. 225-226 (163-165); Chandler's *Of Garryowen in Glory*, pp. 429-430, quotes E. S. Luce's *Keogh, Commanche & Custer*, St. Louis, 1939, pp. 92-96, as 16 officers, 237 enlisted men, 6 civilians and 4 Indian scouts having been killed. Fred Dustin's thorough but somewhat biased study, *The Custer Tragedy*, accounts for one more enlisted man, pp. 225-228, all by name.

July 5 [*sic*]. As I got up this AM, heard a steamboat bell, and in a few minutes the Josephine[96] tied up at the landing. No mail for me.

July 6. Mail came in this AM from Ellis. No mail for me. Capt. [Myles] Moylan and Lieut. [Winfield S.] Edgerly, 7 Cav., dined with us this evening. Had quite a party in the evening at my tent.

July 7. Nothing of interest to note. Mail closed last night at 9, to leave in the AM for Ellis.

July 8. Bradley with two men left at daylight this AM. I hear that he is not to come back until he gets orders to do so.

July 9. Bradley applied to the Genl to go to Shaw, saying his presence there was necessary to his peace of mind. Williamson came in today with mail, bringing letters which had been immersed in the P.P. I spoke to K about George & M. K. [unidentified] Begin drill tomorrow by Co. Evans, Stewart, and Bell went to Crook.[97]

July 10. Capt. Ball came in this AM. Met Bradley at P.P. yesterday. Saw nothing. Our beef cattle strayed off yesterday. Began drill this AM.

July 11. On G[eneral] C[ourts] M[artial]. Met on board the boat, 2 cases. Nothing new. 7 Cav. moved camp late in evening.

July 12. Nothing of interest.

---

96. The steamer *Josephine*, built in 1873, was named after the little daughter of Gen. David S. Stanley. Joseph Mills Hanson, *The Conquest of the Missouri*, Chicago, 1913 (hereafter, *Hanson*), p. 184.

97. These men were all from Co. E, 7th Inf. They were Pvt. James Bell, re-enlisted at Camp Baker, Mont. Territory, July 26, 1875; Pvt. Wm. Evans, St. Louis, April 26, 1875, and Pvt. Benjamin F. Stewart at Newport Barracks, Ky., May 3, 1875. *Muster Roll, Co. E, 7th Inf., Jan.-Feb., 1876, A.G.O., RG 94, N.A.*

July 13. Maj. B told me Reno had in his report of his operations reflected somewhat severely upon the movements of the Montana Column.[98] A shower this PM.

July 14. Sat on Court M. today. Bat[talion] drill in the PM. Men sent across river after horse this PM.

July 15. Herendeen[99] came in last night. Has been to the Crow Camp after scouts; brought 50 who are above the mouth of Big Horn for the night. About midnight there began the most violent thunderstorm I have ever witnessed in this latitude. I left my tent which was under two trees, afraid of lightning. A tree, 20 feet from J. G. tent, was struck, but no injury done. At daylight water from a coulee above camp began to overflow, and in a few minutes everything was under water. Dept. Hd.Qrs. was drowned out. The boat went up for the Indians and returned this AM. Our deserters all came back with some new ones and several squaws. Grasshoppers in myriads made their appearance yesterday. The mail came in from above. Letters from Sallie. Genl Terry has dispatches from Sheridan.[100] The boat began unloading last night.

July 16. Genl Sheridan telegraphs that the Indians must be punished. He can spare no Cav. but will send all the infty. needed. Crook is to

98. While the Reno Report appearing in ***RSW*** 1876, pp. 476-479, does not bear out this statement, Dr. Paulding wrote on July 8, 1876 that Reno's report "reflects strongly on Col. Gibbon . . . for having gone into camp on the evening of the 26th" in the face of the enemy and without attempting to satisfy himself as to the character of a large body of men who crossed his front "or something to that effect." "New Light on the Little Big Horn; Hitherto Unpublished Letters of a Soldier Describing the Stricken Field of the Little Big Horn," *Field Artillery Journal*, XXVI:4(July-August, 1936):356. It may well be that Reno revised his original report.

99. George Herendeen was a citizen-courier residing at Bozeman, Montana Territory. W. A. Graham (ed.), *Official Record of a Court of Inquiry Convened at Chicago, Ill., January 13, 1879, by Request of Major Marcus A. Reno to Investigate His Conduct at the Battle of Little Big Horn, June 25-26, 1876*, Pacific Palisades, Calif., 1951, I, 211.

100. Lt. Gen. Philip H. Sheridan, with headquarters at Chicago, commanded the Division of the Missouri which included the Department of Dakota. ***RSW*** 1876, pp. 25, 439.

join Terry at once. The boat with Terry and staff left this AM. T will return on the Far West.[101]

July 17, Monday. Sat on Court this AM. Spent balance of day in preparing charges against Capt. Sanno who was put in arrest this PM.

July 18. J. G. came to my tent this AM before I had breakfast and at once opened the conversation about S. by asking if I had noticed any change in him since we had been out. I replied that I had not [*sic*] any particular change except that he had lately been more disagreeable than usual. The talk led up to various things, and I told him that I did not think S. had acted as should be expected an officer of his rank and experience should act and cited some cases to him. He agreed with me so far, but said that the matter should be referred to Capt. S. for explanation. I am convinced that he is to be let down as easily as possible. The letter calling upon him for his explanation was a compliment to him and one that he might show with pride to any one. I am very sorry to have felt myself compelled to put charges, but do not think I could act otherwise and retain the respect of the officers of this command which I was fast losing through permitting S to act as he has. The mail came in tonight by McCormick's boat; Cutter[102] came down with it. The posts are to be built after all, and I hear that volunteers are to be called out which, of course, puts an end to reduction of the Army, for the present at least.[103] Mrs. Custer, we hear, is at the point of death from nervous prostration. This has been an excessively warm day, the hottest of the season.

---

101. The steamer *Far West*, built in 1870, was light, strong and speedy. *Hanson*, pp. 238-239.

102. W. Cutter was post trader at Ft. Shaw, Oct. 7, 1870, to April 15, 1871, and at Ft. Ellis beginning July 27, 1871. *Sale of Post Traderships, House Report 799, 44th Cong., 1st Sess.*, Washington, 1876, pp. 272-273.

103. Freeman was speculating of the future here. The bill providing for two additional posts along the Yellowstone was, then, yet to pass Congress. Prior to the Custer disaster a congressional committee had been weighing proposals to reduce the strength of the regular army. *RSW* 1876, pp. 3, 37, 445.

July 19. Maj. Thompson committed suicide at 6AM by shooting himself through the heart with a cal. .44 Colt's revolver. He had been suffering for some days with disease of the kidneys, attended with great pain and was, I suppose, unable to bear it longer.[104] Poor Tompy! He was a gentle, genial man, a thorough gentleman, and his death has cast a gloom over the entire Camp. He was buried at 6:30 PM; all the officers and men of this command attending. Genl G made a few appropriate remarks. [1st Lt. Edward] Maguire read the service. Very warm again today. Far West left.

July 20. An alarm last night about 12 caused by two Indians getting into the 7th Cav. herd. The Crows went out today and found the tracks of about 30 ponies, including two shod horses. Very warm. The boat ought to be in tomorrow.

July 21st. Settled mess bills to June 30. It amounts to $54.29 each. Nothing of interest.

July 22d. Moved Camp ¾ mile below Pease. Weather hot. Mosquitoes awful.[105]

July 23d. Nothing of interest. Awfully hot and plenty of mosquitoes. Wheelan left for below on 5 day scout this AM.

July 24. Mosquitoes and heat last night. Slept but little. Face larged up with toothache this AM. Maj. Reno put in arrest by D. G. [Gen.

---

104. Captain Thompson had suffered from neuralgia and nervous prostration for years as a result of his confinement in Libby Prison, Richmond, during the war until, rendered desperate by his sufferings, he put an end to his existence by shooting himself. Barry C. Johnson (ed.), "Dr. Paulding and His Remarkable Diary," *Sidelights of the Sioux Wars*, London, 1967, p. 63; *Gibbon*, p. 677. Freeman may well have become acquainted with Thompson at Libby for both wefe imprisoned there in 1864. Willard W. Glazier, *The Capture, the Prison Pen, the Escape*, New York, 1868, p. 369.

105. Rufus F. Zogbaum, *Horse, Foot & Dragoons*, New York, 1888, p. 127, doubts if one can ever become hardened to the sting of a Montana mosquito.

Officers and Their Families at Ft. Fred Steele, Wyoming, about 1885. *Standing, left to right:* Capt. L. F. Burnett, 7th Inf.; Lt. G. W. McIver, 7th Inf.; Lt. Col. H. L. Chipman, 7th Inf., post commander; Capt. T. S. Kirtland, 7th Inf.; Lt. H. D. Styer, 21st Inf.; Lt. L. D. Greene, 7th Inf.; Capt. W. I. Reed, 7th Inf.; and Capt. Daniel Weisel, Medical Corps. *Sitting, left to right:* Lt. W. Wittich, 21st Inf.; Mrs. Kirtland; L. Cutler; Mrs. Chipman; R. Cutler; others not identified. (Capts. Burnett, Kirtland and Reed are mentioned in the Freeman journal.) (*Courtesy of U. S. Army Signal Corps and National Archives.*)

Gibbon] this AM. Nothing else of news. Wrote letters to Rob, wife and boys.[106]

July 25. A courier from Capt. Wheelan said the boat with Genl. Terry would be up today, but she stopped about 6 miles below tonight. She had to leave 60 tons near the mouth of Little Porcupine. A man of 7 Cav. was drowned this AM, crossing a slough swollen by the rains of the past two days. His body not yet recovered. The three men who carried the message to Crook[107] returned this evening. Bring letters from [Capt. Anson] Mills [3rd Cav.] to me and two from [Capt. Andrew S.] Burt [9th Inf.] to the Genl. They are on Goose Creek and are anxious to join us, have made 4 attempts to communicate with us. J. G. is very anxious I should withdraw the charges against S. I sent in a letter with the conditions upon which I would do so this PM.

July 26. Boat arrived this AM. Preparation mounting for a move. Charges against S. returned, say conditions complied with. Nothing else of interest.

July 27. Left Camp at 10AM. Boat left at 9. Marched about 6 miles. Very warm. Mail left this AM.

July 28. Marched 16¾ miles. Plenty of water today but very warm. Camped ½-mile from our camp going up.

July 29. Marched 23 miles, camped near spring.

July 30. Marched 18 miles to Rosebud. ~~31 Aug~~ [*sic*]

---

106. At this time the Freeman's had two sons, Reese Darlington, age eight, and Louis, four. *Army and Navy Journal*, XX, Whole No. 1007 (Dec. 9, 1882), p. 414; Extract copy, *Hennepin Co., Minn. Census of 1880, Records of the Bureau of the Census, Pittsburg, Kans.*

107. See entry of July 9, footnote 97.

Aug. 2. Lay in Camp from 30 till this AM. Co. went on Carrol[108] as escort to Powder River with Forsyth.[109] Up 30 miles from P.R.

Aug 3. Met Far West and ~~rations~~ [*sic*] transferred to her.

Aug. 4. Arrived in Camp at Rosebud. Found command crossed to south bank. Staid on boat until night and went into camp with the battalion.

Aug. 5. Spent the day in regulating baggage which has been cut down and in trying to buy commissary stores. Took dinner on the boat.

Aug. 6, Sunday. Sat on court for trial of [2nd] Lt. [James E.] Macklin, 22d Inf., for drunkenness on duty. Court met on boat and had dinner.

Aug. 7. Sat on court today on S[team] B[oat] Josephine for the trial of [2nd] Lt. [Jas. H.] Whitten, 5th Inf., for drunkenness. Had dinner on boat. Inf. brigade under J. G.; [Col. Nelson A.] Miles [5th Inf.] and [Maj. Orlando H.] Moore [6th Inf.], right wing; [Lt. Col. Elwell S.] Otis [22nd Inf.] & Freeman, left wing. Start at 5AM tomorrow. 1st Indian Scouts, 2d Bat. Cav., 3 Battery, 3 Cav., 4 ambulances, HdQrs train, right train, supply train. Bat. Cav., Inf. on either flank. Beef herd beside the train. Wrote letter to Sallie.

Aug. 8. Left Camp at 5AM, marched 10 miles up Rosebud. No Indian sign.

---

108. There were a number of Missouri River steamboats bearing this name. This *Carroll* was chartered for army use from July 24 to Sept. 20, 1876, at a cost of from $300 to $360 per day. *South Dakota Historical Collections*, XXVI (1952), Ralph E. Nichol, "Steamboat Navigation on the Missouri River with Special Reference to Yankton and Vicinity," p. 200; *RSW* 1877, p. 311.

109. Major Jas. W. Forsyth, 10th Cav., military secretary to General Sheridan. Edgar I. Stewart (ed.), *Field Diary of Lt. Edward S. Godfrey*, Portland, 1962, p. 70; *Army Register*, 1880, p. 111.

Aug. 9. Marched 11 miles. No Indian signs. Courier sent out last night reports plenty of Indians 30 miles up this stream. Sioux reported in Camp last night. New courier started to Crook.

Aug. 10. Left Camp at 5AM, marched about 5 miles. Courier sent out last night came rushing back and reported a heap of Sioux coming close. Train parked; disposition for fight made. Troops deployed, &c. Soon found it was Crook's command. Marched 15 miles and camped with Crook. The 5 Infty. goes back to the river, then takes the boats and goes down river to watch the crossings. We unite with Crook and follow the Indians who are certainly on Tongue or Powder River, if they have not already crossed north. I think Old S[itting] B[ull][110] will ~~th~~ [*sic*] conclude the country is alive with white soldiers when he sees us come.

Aug. 11. Left Camp on Rosebud at 11AM and marched until 6PM, about 12 miles across and then 3 miles down. Big trail but old. Fine road. Steep bluff on Tongue. Dead white man found today and the remains of another who is supposed to have been burned at the stake. Tongue River is a quite clear stream with a fine valley at this point. Met Burt last night; he wants a Bat.

Aug. 12. Rained all night and, at 8AM, bids fair to do so all day. Did rain all day. Started at 11AM, marched down Tongue, camped at 6. Forded river 3 times. Marched 13 miles.

Aug. 13. Left Camp at 7AM, marched down Tongue 25+ miles, camped about 5 miles from mouth. 3 men missing tonight from the 6th Infty. Scouts went to Yellow[*sic*].

---

110. Sitting Bull had become widely known among both red and white men as the champion of traditional Indian customs. He was a medicine man and a chief, but not a warrior chief. He held the highest rank possible in his own tribe. *Stewart*, pp. 184-187.

Aug. 14. Left Camp at 5AM, marched down Tongue then 8 miles up a creek on trail to Powder and camped. Rainwater. Sioux seem to be living on their horses and roots. Scouts returned from Yellowstone, saw Miles and S boat. [1st Lt. Wm. I.] Reed [Co. E, 7th Inf.], [1st Lt. Wm. Philo] Clark [2nd Cav.],[111] and [2nd Lt. Francis] Woodbridge [Co. A, 7th Inf.], with 250 Crows are on the way, supposed to be at Tongue River tonight. Sioux still on this side of river.

Aug. 15. Left Camp at 6AM. We left Pumpkin Creek, upon which we camped last night, crossed divide to Mizpah Creek which we followed down to Powder. Marched 20¼. Find the trail goes down.

Aug. 16. Left Camp at 6AM, marched down 19¾ miles. Rain at Camp. No fresh sign. Nothing new. Capt. [Archibald H.] Goodloe, 22d, had stroke of paralysis today.

Aug. 17. Marched 23 miles to Yellowstone. Trail turns east to L[ittle] Miss[ouri]. Crossed Powder twice unnecessarily. Boat up river, came this eve[ning]. Woodruff and Reed here. Ten letters.

Aug. 18. Lay in Camp preparing for march. This evening General T told me we would not move until we got more rations. Messengers sent to bring SB up from below. Moved Camp about 1 mile.

Aug. 19. Boat came in this PM and started at once for Rosebud. All sorts of rumors are flying around in regard to future movements.

20 21. Still in Camp. Carroll, with [1st Lt. Allen H.] Jackson [Co. K, 7th Inf.] on board, came in this evening. Now said we will move on 23d.

---

111. Clark was an authority on the Indian sign language and had published a work by that title, Philadelphia, 1885. W. E. Graham, *Custer Myth*, Harrisburg, 1953, p. 80.

22-3-4. Quietly waiting the word to move. Far West came down early yesterday AM and went to ferrying. Took some clothes out of train, &c. Fleet, with [Capt. Louis H.] Sanger [17th Inf.] and baggage left at Rosebud, came in about 4PM. Scout came in from [Capt. Edmund] Rice, 5th Infantry, yesterday, saying large force of Indians crossed to N side Yellowstone at or near Glendive.[112] Rain for past three days, very hard last night. Drowned everything out. Was dripping wet this AM. Have drawn rations 3 times. Order out to march in the AM at 6.

Aug. 25. Left Camp at 6AM. Were delayed nearly an hour by the 5 Inf. Marched 18 miles out, camped near mouth of small creek emptying to Powder. Courier from boat says 10 boats have arrived at Powder, 4 Cos. 5[th Inf.] and supplies. Indians fighting Rice at Glendive, wounded 3 men on boat. Crook camped 7 miles above. Lots of rumors tonight. [*indecipherable*]

Aug. 26. Left Camp at 6AM. Train and 6[th Inf.] go back to [*unintelligible*] with Terry. Will cross train and troops. Terry goes to Glendive with the 5 cos. 5[th Inf.]. Crook follows trail. We marched 22 miles and camped on Yellowstone 8 miles below Powder. Had considerable difficulty in getting down the bluffs to river.

Aug. 27. Ferried whole command across river on Steamers Yellowstone[113] & Carroll. Genl T and staff came down on boat. We lay on the bank until 5PM. We struck out north, marched 5 miles. Made dry camp. I understand the object of this move is to cut off and surround Indians who are troubling Rice.

---

112. Captain Rice was in command of troops guarding supplies at the mouth of Glendive Creek. *Hanson*, p. 340.

113. A sidewheeler steamer of 378 tons. John E. Parsons, "Steamboats in the Idaho Gold Rush," *Montana, the Magazine of Western History*, X:1(Jan. 1960) (hereafter, *Parsons*):54.

Aug. 28. Left Camp at 5AM. Found water holes on creek about 3 miles from Camp. Stopped to cook breakfast. Went on at 9AM. Hot day. No water except in pools. Men suffered some for water. Camped on same stream, "Bad Route Creek." 25 miles by map to head of dry V. Splendid grass; good water tonight.

Aug. 29. Left Camp at 6AM, marched 17 miles to sight of Missouri waters, turned to right and camped on dry creek with water holes. Found good water by digging. Marched NE then due east. Immense amount of shooting, killed several buffalo. Plenty of meat in Camp. 4 Cos. Cav. went on divide toward Musselshell to look for Indians. Capt. Logan lost his horse and complete outfit.

Aug. 30. Left Camp at 6AM, continued eastward movement. Marched 17¾ mi. Camped on Deer Creek.

Aug. 31st. Left Camp at 7AM, marched 13 miles to Yellowstone. Reno out on 4 days scout.

Sept. 1st, 2. In Camp. Train came this AM. Hear that our Co. wagons at Powder have been unloaded and contents scattered. 2 Cos. of 5th came up from the Benton.[114] Far West passed down; reports very low water on Wolf Rapids. Doubtful if more boats can get up. Woodruff gets his leave when the expedition breaks up, which J. G. told me last night would be soon if nothing special occurred to prevent it.

Sept. 5. Woodruff and English left on Yellowstone on leave. Order dissolving expedition out this PM. March at 8AM, 6th. Spent the evening at Genl T's HeadQrs., singing and a general goodbye.

---

114. Steamer *Benton* was a sternwheeler of 246 tons, built at McKeesport, Penn. *Parsons*, p. 54.

Sept. 6. Left Camp at 10:20AM with 30 wagons loaded with rations for our march to Ellis and supplies for the new posts. Marched 14 miles partly over hills. Good camp on creek 3 mi. from river. Genl T came to bid us goodbye, very polite, &c. 5PM. 2 Cos. of 22d Inf. came in Stockade Creek.[115]

Sept. 7. Left Camp at 6AM, made 15 miles to Bad Route Creek. Men on side of the road. Hard marching. Halted 2 hours. Good wood, water and grass. Marched on at 3PM in a drenching rain. Cold; men wet through. Rained nearly all night. Got in Camp at dark. Wood scarce. Caught severe cold.

Sept. 8. Left Camp at 6AM, marched 16 mi. Camped on Cherry Creek early. Cool in AM; good sun PM. Dried blankets, &c. Met Sanger with train at 10AM. Took 2 ⟨R⟩ wagons from him.

Sept. 9. Left Camp at 6AM. Cool, pleasant, marched 30 miles to mouth of Custer Creek to trains. Found our property left at Rosebud in bad fix. Many of the men lost their blankets and clothing. Woodruff's mess chest and contents missing. Route from here to Glendive through good country most of the way; grass & water plenty. Little timber from here to Cherry Creek. Bad lands between road & river.

Sept. 10. Drew 10 days rations. Left Camp at 12M. Jacobs left clothing instead of issuing it to the men who needed it very much.[116] Marched 9 miles, road through bad lands. Most of the way very bad. Camped just below S[team] B[oat] Point.

---

115. Cos. G, H, K, and I, 22nd Inf. established a cantonment at Glendive Creek, as the falling river prevented further navigation that year and necessitated unloading supplies. *RSW* 1877, pp. 309, 487.

116. *Bradley*, pp. 216-217 (146), too, voiced dissatisfaction with Jacobs' efforts as quartermaster, but on another occasion. However, the lot of the quartermaster, like that of the policeman, was not a happy one.

Sept. 11. Train did not get in until after dark last night. This AM took 2,000 lbs. off the ⟨R⟩ teams which was put on the Co. wagons. [Capt. Simon] Snyder's Co. [F, 5th Inf.] crossed Steamboat Point in 45 min. The 7th used two hours going by the road. At 12 passed [Capt. Andrew S.] Bennet's Co. [B] 5th [Inf.] at Buffalo Rapids. Camped at 4:30 on Difficult Creek. Marched about 20 miles.

Sept. 12. Left Camp at 7AM, marched 7 miles. Camped opposite Post No. 1.[117] Brewer [unidentified] came into Camp last night. Said arrangements to pay off the mortgage on his place had been made. Att[orne] y did not sue for costs, a mistake for which I suppose I will have to pay.

Sept. 13. Left Camp at 7. Inf. made cut-off from Camp to creek. Marched 21 miles. Camped at mouth Coal Creek.

Sept. 14. Marched 22 miles to Little Porcupine Creek. Met nine pilgrims.[118]

Sept. 15. Marched 19 miles, camped at 2PM. Killed beef.

Sept. 16. Marched about 18 miles, camped on the ground of our 2d camp from Pease last May.

Sept. 17. Marched 22½ miles, camped on bottom above Big Horn.

Sept. 19. Lay over yesterday. Men washed, &c. Left Camp this AM, marched 25 miles.

---

117. Post No. 1 was also referred to as the Tongue River Cantonment. A little later as Ft. Keogh it was located about 1½ miles above the mouth of the Tongue River. *Reports of Inspection Made in Summer of 1877 . . . North of Union Pacific R.R.*, Washington, 1878, pp. 5, 27, 63; *Heitman*, II, 514, 551, and Francis Paul Prucha, *Guide to the Military Posts of the U.S.*, Madison, 1964, p. 82.

118. Term applied to newcomers. *Stewart*, pp. 387-388.

Sept. 20. Left Camp at 6, 8 miles to P.P. Made cut-off with men to river, 8 miles from B.B.G. Wagons in late. Bad camp. Taylor tells me there is water on left of road going down at some white clay banks, 2 miles beyond wooden fort, and in meadow 8 miles from river on top of ridge this side.

Sept. 21. Issued rations. Left Camp at 9AM, marched 7½ miles and stopped to noon at 12. Left at 2:30, marched 1½ miles, camped at B.B.G. Went after trout but caught ten skipjacks. Wrote home. Road going down can be considerably shortened by keeping to left on bench. Hoffman,[119] K Co., buried here tonight.

Sept. 22d. Left Camp at 6:20, marched until 3PM, about 22 miles to Clark's Fork. Caught 15 trout.

Sept. 23. Marched 20¾ to supply camp.

Sept. 24. Marched to ford 6 miles above Countryman's, 19 miles. Can't cross.

Sept. 25. Marched 17 miles to Spring 6 miles from Sweetgrass. Mail and grain from Ellis.

Sept. 26. Marched 17 miles to Otter Creek. Left the Ellis road. Marched 5 miles up Otter, 22 miles.

Sept. 27. Marched 20 miles, camped at leaving of Sweetgrass. Good grass.

Sept. 28. Marched 24 miles to Big Elk. Got on wrong road and went 6 to 8 miles out of the way.

---

119. Pvt. Sumner W. Hoffman, Co. K, 7th Inf., enlisted at Chicago, March 23, 1873, died of Camp Fever at camp near Yellowstone, M. T., September 20, 1876. *Muster Roll, Co. K, 7th Inf., Sept.-Oct., 1876, A.G.O., RG 94, N.A.*

Sept. 29. Marched 22 miles, camped near [Fort] Howe, 3 miles.[120] Logan found his horse.[121]

Sept. 30. Marched 25 miles, camped on 4-Mile above Reid's Ranch.[122]

Oct. 1st. Left Camp at 6AM, camped at [Hot] Springs at 8AM.

Oct. 2d. Marched 17 miles, camped at [Camp] Baker at 12M. Letter from Sallie. Dined with Mrs. Gilbert [wife of Lt. Col. Chas. C. Gilbert, 7th Inf., commanding Camp Baker].

Oct 3. Marched to Cottonwood. Men drunk. Broke and upset co. wagon.

Oct. 4. Camped half way between the Hound Creeks. Wagons late.

Oct. 5. Camped on Shaw side of Mo. River.

Oct. 6. Reached home at 2PM. Here endith [*sic*] the Sioux Campaign for us.

---

120. Probably Ft. Howie, a stockade erected by the Montana militia mobilized by Gov. Thomas F. Meagher in 1867. Neil Howie was a Helena major of militia. *Bradley*, p. 152 (29); *Memoirs*, p. 18, and John S. Gray, "Northern Overland Pony Express," *Montana, the Magazine of Western History*, XVI:4(Oct., 1966):62,65.

121. Logan had lost his horse and equipment a month previously. See entry for August 29.

122. Granville Stuart (*Forty Years on the Frontier*, Glendale, 1957, II, 134) in 1880 located "Reeds place" somewhat northeast of the area in which Freeman was traveling in 1876.

BIBLIOGRAPHY

BIBLIOGRAPHY

MANUSCRIPTS

Bureau of the Census,
Census of 1880 (extracts),
Ft. Snelling, Hennepin Co., Minn.
Rawlins, Carbon Co., Wyo.

Carey, Mrs. Robert D. (*nee* Julia Freeman),
Correspondence, various dates during 1963.

Department of the Army, Office of the Chief of Military History,
Diary of Dr. Holmes Offley Paulding (copy furnished).

National Archives,
War Department, Adjutant General's Office, Record Group 94,
Muster Roll, Co. H, 7th Infantry, Jan. - Feb. 1876; Sept. - Oct. 1876,
" " " K, 7th Infantry, July - Aug. 1876; Sept. - Oct. 1876,
" " " E, 7th Infantry, Jan. - Feb. 1876,
" " " H, 2nd Cavalry, March - April, 1876.

Register of Enlistments, U.S. Army, Vol. 54-55 (A-K) 1859-1863, p. 45.

Service Papers of Henry Blanchard Freeman.

Pension Bureau, Record Group 15, T-288, Roll 163,
Widow's Pension Application (Freeman, Henry Blanchard – widow Sarah E., dated Dec. 23, 1915) No. 1, 057,758
Certificate No. 807,279.

Wyoming State Archives and Historical Dept.,
Correspondence various dates during 1963.

Yale University Library, Coe Collection,
Homer Coon's Recollections, (Withington No. 110), microfilm,
William English Journal (Withington No. 171), copy,
H. B. Freeman Journal (Withington No. 204), microfilm.

PUBLISHED DOCUMENTS

Adjutant General's Office, *Army Register*, annually 1867-1880, Washington,

Revised U.S. Army Regulations of 1861, Revised to June 25, 1863, Washington, 1863.

Department of the Army, *The Medal of Honor*, Washington, 1948.

Graham, W. A. (ed.) *Official Record of a Court of Inquiry Convened at Chicago, Illinois, January 13, 1879, by Request of Major Marcus A. Reno to Investigate His Conduct at the Battle of Little Big Horn, June 25-26, 1876*, Pacific Palisades, 1951.

Heitman, Francis B., *Historical Register and Dictionary of the U.S. Army*, Washington, 1903.

Hodge, Frederick Webb, *Handbook of the American Indians North of Mexico*, Washington, Smithsonian Institution, Bureau of American Ethnology, Bulletin No. 30, 1905 (Reprint, New York, 1959).

Lieber, Guido Norman, *Remarks on the Army Regulations*, Washington, 1898.

Reports of Inspection Made in the Summer of 1877 by Gen. P. H. Sheridan & W. T. Sherman of Country North of the Union Pacific Railroad, Washington, 1878.

Report of the Secretary of the Interior, 1876 and 1877, Washington, 1876 and 1877.

Report of the Secretary of War, 1867, 1872 and 1876, Washington, as indicated.

Report of the Chief Engineer, Part III, Appendix 00 to Report of Secretary of War, 1876, Washington, 1876.

U. S. Congress, House Report No. 799, Forty-fourth Congress, First Session,

Senate Executive Document No. 52, Forty-fourth Congress, First Session,

Senate Executive Document No. 19, Forty-sixth Congress, Third Session.

BOOKS

Bradley, James H., *The March of the Montana Column: A Prelude to the Custer Disaster* (reprint of "The Journal of Lt. James H. Bradley," edited by Edgar I. Stewart), Norman, Oklahoma University Press, 1961.

Brown, Mark H., *The Plainsmen of the Yellowstone: A History of the Yellowstone Basin*, New York, G. P. Putnam's Sons, 1961.

Birkhimer, William Edward, *Historical Sketch of the Organization, Administration, Material and Tactics of the Artillery, U.S. Army*, Washington, James J. Chapman, Agent, 1884.

Boatner, Mark H., *Civil War Dictionary*, New York, David McKay Co., 1959.

Bourke, John G., *On the Border with Crook*, New York, Charles Scribner's Sons, 1891.

Carrington, Frances Courtney, *My Army Life and the Fort Phil Kearney Massacre*, Philadelphia, J. B. Lippincott Co., 1910.

Carrington, Margaret I., *Ab-Sa-Ra-Ka, Land of Massacre*, Philadelphia, J. B. Lippincott Co., 1878.

Chandler, Melbourne C., *Of Garryowen in Glory: The History of the 7th U. S. Cavalry*, Annadale, 7th Cavalry Assn., 1960.

Clark, William Philo, *Indian Sign Language: With Brief Explanatory Notes, etc.*, Philadelphia, L. R. Hamersly & Co., 1885.

Dion, James H., "History of Banking in Montana," in *A History of Montana*, Vol. I (ed. Merrill G. Burlingame & K. Ross Toole), New York, Lewis Historical Pub. Co. Inc., 1957.

Dustin, Fred, *The Custer Tragedy*, Ann Arbor, Mich., Edwards Bros., 1939. (Reprint, 1965).

———, *Echoes from the Little Big Horn Fight: Reno's Position in the Valley*, Saginaw, privately printed, 1953.

Eggenhofer, Nick, *Wagons, Mules and Men: How the Frontier Moved West*, New York, Hastings, 1961.

Farrow, Edward S., *Military Encyclopedia* (3 vols.), New York, privately printed, 1885.

Glazier, Willard W., *The Capture, the Prison Pen, and the Escape, giving a Complete History of Prison Life in the South*, New York, Ferguson, 1870 (1868).

Graham, William A., *Abstract of the Official Record of Proceedings of the Reno Court of Inquiry . . .* , Harrisburg, Stackpole Co., 1954.

———, *The Custer Myth: A Source Book of Custeriana*, Harrisburg, Stackpole Co., 1953.

———, *Custer's Battle Flags*, Hollywood, privately printed, 1952. (Originally appeared in 1950 Los Angeles Westerners' *Brand Book*.)

Hanson, Joseph Mills, *The Conquest of the Missouri: Being the Story of the Life and Exploits of Capt. Grant Marsh*, Chicago, A. C. McClurg & Co., 1913.

Hebard, Grace R. and E. A. Brininstool, *Bozeman Trail* (2 vols.), Cleveland, Arthur H. Clark Co., 1922.

Hunt, Frazier and Robert Hunt, *I Fought with Custer: The Story of Sergeant Charles Windolph*, New York, Charles Scribner's Sons, 1947.

Johnson, A. B., "The 7th Regiment of Infantry," in *The Army of the United States* (ed. Theo. F. Rodenbough and William L. Haskin), New York, privately printed, 1896.

Jones, Robert Hugh, *Civil War in the Northwest*, Norman, Oklahoma University Press, 1960.

Kuhlman, Charles, *Legend into History: the Custer Mystery*, Harrisburg, Stackpole Co., 1951.

Marquis, Thomas B., *Memoirs of a White Crow Indian (Thomas H. LeForge)*, New York, Century Co., 1928.

———, *Wooden Leg: A Warrior Who Fought Custer*, Lincoln, Nebraska University Press, 1957 (reprint of *A Warrior Who Fought Custer (the Narrative of Wooden Leg)*, Minneapolis, Midwest Pub. Co., 1931.

Mattes, Merrill J., *Indians, Infants and Infantry: Andrew and Elizabeth Burt on the Frontier*, Denver, Old West Pub. Co., 1960.

Mills, Anson, *My Story*, Washington, privately printed, 1918.

National Cyclopaedia of American Biography: Being the History of the U.S., New York, James T. White, 1907

Ostrander, Anson B., *After Sixty Years*, Seattle, privately printed, 1925.

———, *An Army Boy of the Sixties*, Yonkers, privately printed, 1924.

Parsons, John E. and John S. duMont, *Firearms in the Custer Battle*, Harrisburg, Stackpole Co., 1953.

Phillips, Paul C. (ed.), *Forty Years on the Frontier as Seen in the Journals and Reminiscences of Granville Stuart*, Glendale, Arthur H. Clark Co., 1957. (Reprint of 1925 edition, same publisher but Cleveland.)

——— and Llewellyn L. Callaway, *Medicine in the Making of Montana*, Missoula, Montana Medical Assn., 1962.

Prucha, Francis Paul, S. J., *Guide to the Military Posts of the U.S.*, Madison, State Historical Society of Wisconsin, 1964.

Quaife, W. M. (ed.), *"Yellowstone Kelly," The Memoirs of Luther S. Kelly*, New Haven, Yale University Press, 1926.

Roe, Charles F., *Custer's Last Battle*, New York, privately printed, 1927.

Roe, Frances M. A., *Army Letters from an Officer's Wife, 1871-1888*, New York, D. Appleton & Co., 1909.

Russell, Carl P., *Guns on the Early Frontier*, Berkeley & Los Angeles, University of California Press, 1957.

Schmidt, Martin F. (ed.), *General George Crook: His Autobiography*, Norman, Oklahoma University Press, 1946.

Schoenberg, Wilfred P., S. J., *Chronicle of Catholic History of Pacific Northwest, 1743-1960*, Portland, privately printed, 1962.

Scudder, Ralph E., *Custer Country*, Portland, Binfords & Mort, 1963.

Stanley, David S., *Personal Memoirs*, Cambridge, Harvard University Press, 1917.

Steckmesser, Kent Ladd, *The Western Hero in History and Legend*, Norman, Oklahoma University Press, 1965.

Stewart, Edgar I. (ed.), *Bradley's March . . .* (which see).

————, *Custer's Luck*, Norman, Oklahoma University Press, 1955.

———— and Jane Stewart (eds.), *Field Diary of Lt. Edward S. Godfrey, Commanding Co. K, 7th Cavalry Regiment under Lt. Col. Custer at the Little Big Horn*, Portland, Champoeg Press, 1962.

Van de water, Frederic P., *Glory Hunter: A Life of General Custer*, Indianapolis, Bobbs-Merrill, 1934.

Zogbaum, Rufus F., *Horse, Foot and Dragoon: Sketches of Army Life at Home and Abroad*, New York, Harper & Bros., 1888.

PERIODICALS

Bradley, James H., "The Journal of . . . ," *Contributions to the Historical Society of Montana*, II, 1896, pp. 140-228.

Brown, Mark H., "Muddled Men Have Muddled the Yellowstone's True Color," *Montana, the Magazine of Western History*, XI:1(Winter, 1961):28-37.

———— "A New Focus on the Sioux War," *Montana, the Magazine of Western History*, XI:4(Autumn, 1961):76-85.

Burlingame, Merrill G., "The Andrew Jackson Hunter Family-Mary Hunter Doane," *The Montana Magazine of History*, I:1(Jan., 1958):5-13.

Carroll, Matthew, "Diary of . . . ," *Contributions to the Historical Society of Montana*, II, 1896, pp. 229-240.

"Commuter's Quandry," a reprint from *Montana Post*, October 16, 1868, *Montana, the Magazine of Western History*, IV:3(Summer, 1954):51.

Coughlan, T. M., "The Battle of the Little Big Horn: A Tactical Study," *Cavalry Journal*, XLIII:181(Jan.-Feb. 1934):13-20.

Deland, Charles E., "The Sioux Wars," *South Dakota Historical Collections*, XV (1930), pp. 9-730; XVII (1934), pp. 177-551.

Eberstadt, Edward, "The William Robertson Coe Collection of Western Americana," *Yale University Library Gazette*, XXIII:2(Oct., 1948):37-130.

Foster, James S., "Outlines of History of the Territory of Dakota and Emigrants' Guide . . . of the West," Yankton, D. T. 1870 (reprint, *South Dakota Historical Collections*, XIV [1928], pp. 71-180).

Gibbon, John, "Hunting Sitting Bull," *American Catholic Quarterly Review*, II:(Sept., 1877):665-694.

———— "Last Summer's Expedition Against the Sioux," *American Catholic Quarterly Review*, II:(April, 1877):271-304.

Godfrey, Edward Settle, "Custer's Last Battle," *Century Magazine*, XLIII:3 (Jan. 1892):358-387; also, *Contributions to the Historical Society of Montana*, IX(1923):141-225.

Gray, John S., "Northern Overland Pony Express," *Montana, the Magazine of Western History*, XVI:4(Oct., 1966):58-76.

Johnson, Barry C. (ed.), "Dr. Paulding and His Remarkable Diary," *Sidelights of the Sioux Wars* (Special Publication No. 2, London, English Westerners Society, 1967), pp. 47-69.

McClernand, Edward J., "With the Indian and Buffalo in Montana," *Cavalry Journal*, XXXVI:146(Jan., 1927):7-53.

McLemore, Clyde, "Fort Pease, The First Attempted Settlement in Yellowstone Valley," *The Montana Magazine of History*, II:1(Jan., 1952):16-32.

Murray, Robert A., "Artillery Against the Northern Plains Indians, 1823-1890," *Gun Report*, XIII:5(Oct., 1967):18-29.

Nichol, Ralph E., "Steamboat Navigation on the Missouri River with Special Reference to Yanktown and Vicinity," *South Dakota Historical Collections*, XXVI (1952), pp. 181-221.

Nye, Elwood L., "Marching with Custer," *Army Veterinary Bulletin*, XXXV:2 (Apr., 1941):114-140.

Parsons, John E., "Steamboats in the Idaho Gold Rush," *Montana, the Magazine of Western History*, X:1(Jan., 1960):51-61.

Paulding, Holmes Offley, "New Light on the Little Big Horn," *Field Artillery Journal*, XXVI:4(July-Aug., 1936):343-360.

Robinson, Doane, "The Rescue of Frances Kelly," *South Dakota Historical Collections*, IV (1908), pp. 109-117.

Robinson, Will, "Commissioner of Indian Affairs Reports as Pertains to the Sioux and other Indians of Dakota Territory Digest," *South Dakota Historical Collections*, XXIX (1958), pp. 307-500.

Sharp, Paul F., "Merchant Princes of the Plains," *Montana, the Magazine of History*, V:1(Winter, 1955):2-20.

Stewart, Edgar I., "The Reno Court of Inquiry," *The Montana Magazine of History*, II:3(July, 1952):31-43.

Walton, George H., "The Tart-tongued Bomb Thrower of the 7th Cavalry," *Army*, XV:1(Aug., 1964):62-64.

NEWSPAPERS

Army and Navy Journal, LIII:8(Oct. 23, 1915) obituary notice.
XX:19(Dec. 9, 1882):414.

Yates Center News, (Yates Center, Kans.) Friday, June 23, 1882.

INDEX

INDEX

(All military rank listed is actual contemporary rank; wartime and brevet rank being disregarded.)